World War II Histories and Reports

World War II Histories and Reports

A Partial Checklist

© Ross & Perry, Inc. 2001 All rights reserved.

No claim to U.S. government work contained throughout this book.

Protected under the Berne Convention. Published 2001

Printed in The United States of America
Ross & Perry, Inc. Publishers
717 Second St., N.E., Suite 200
Washington, D.C. 20002
Telephone (202) 675-8300
Facsimile (202) 675-8400
info@RossPerry.com

SAN 253-8555

Government Reprints Press Edition 2001

Government Reprints Press is an Imprint of Ross & Perry, Inc.

Previously printed as "World War II Histories and Historical Reports in the Naval History Division" by Operational Archives, Naval History Division.

Library of Congress Control Number: 2001093134

http://www.GPOreprints.com

ISBN 1-931641-37-4

⊚ The paper used in this publication meets the requirements for permanence established by the American National Standard for Information Sciences "Permanence of Paper for Printed Library Materials" (ANSI Z39.48-1984).

All rights reserved. No copyrighted part of this publication may be reproduced, stored in a retrieval system, or transmitted, in any form or by any means, electronic, photocopying, recording, or otherwise, without the prior written permission of the publisher.

FOREWORD

The purpose of this annotated checklist is to facilitate research by officials and scholars in one of the groups of special information resources held by the Naval History Division, and to supplement the generalized descriptions of such holdings that are contained in the publication, U. S. Naval History Sources in the Washington Area and Suggested Research Subjects. The current project was undertaken jointly by staff members of this Division and by a number of Naval Reservists who had brief tours of active duty for training with our organization.

The histories and historical reports described in this catalogue relate primarily to the operations and administration of naval commands during the World War II era. In addition, some histories from other services or agencies are included, and in a few cases coverage is provided of pre-World War II and post-war events. Although limited numbers of privately prepared accounts are included, the material was predominantly official in origin. For the most part, these documents were originally security-classified, but all documents are now declassified. The majority of the accounts are in typescript or mimeographed form, although a few entries refer to printed editions that originally were circulated within the Navy as classified publications.

Unless otherwise indicated, all documents are located in the World War II Command File of the Naval History Division's Operational Archives. A small number of the entries (identified in the citations as "Admin. Hist. Appen.") are part of a separate collection of documentation forwarded as appendices to the administrative histories of major World War II commands.

The specific location of the histories in these files is indicated in each citation.

It should be emphasized that this catalogue is <u>not</u> a complete list of all of the unpublished or limited-circulation histories relating to the World War II era that are included in Naval History Division collections. Among our additional holdings is a group of some 350 bound volumes in the Navy Department Library representing the administrative histories of major World War II commands. In addition, the Operational Archives has a large group of aviation-unit histories, and the Division's Ship History Branch has an extensive collection of World War II ship histories.

The following Naval Reserve personnel undertook the basic work on this checklist: LT Charles C. Chadbourn, III; LT Dan Cromack; LCDR Alexander S. Daley; LT Danny M. Dixon; CDR Wallace S. Hutcheon; LCDR Lawrence J. Korb; LT Joseph C. Kudless; TM1 (SS) Robert L. Lookabill; LT Christopher A. Peterson; LT Michael E. Phelps; LT Michael R. Rudy; LT Roderick S. Speer; LTJG Jeffrey P. Sweetland; and CE2 Philip B. Wortman. Their efforts were supported and supplemented by the following staff members of this Division: LCDR Richard W. MacKay, USN, Mr. Edward J. Marolda, Miss Mary M. Wonders, and Mrs. Jeanette A. Koontz. The overall project was directed by Dr. Dean C. Allard and Mrs. Kathleen M. Lloyd of the Operational Archives.

All of the items appearing in this checklist are available for use in the Naval History Division. Arrangements also can be made to purchase photocopies of official histories. When microfilm copies of the documents are already on hand, these films are available for circulation within the inter-library loan system.

Individuals desiring to inquire about loans or photocopying are invited to correspond with the Operational
Archives.

                                    EDWIN B. HOOPER
                                    Vice Admiral, USN (Ret.)
                                    Director of Naval History

TABLE OF CONTENTS

	PAGE
FOREWORD	iii
ANNOTATED CHECKLIST	1
GLOSSARY OF ABBREVIATIONS	184
SUBJECT INDEX	191

A

1. Acorn Thirteen, "History of Acorn Thirteen." Admin. Hist. Appen. SoPac Admin. Hist. 75, 16 November 1944. 56 pp. Appendices, photographs.

   This account is divided into three parts: 1) an overall narrative, 2) a chronology, and 3) an appendix with photographs. An "acorn" was a unit designed to consolidate and develop advanced bases for use by aircraft service units supporting fleet air squadrons.

2. Air Force Evaluation Board, Pacific Ocean Area, "Report Number III, The Occupation of Leyte, Philippine Islands." Air Force, 1944. 76 pp. Maps, illustrations.

   This report on the effectiveness of close air support rendered by Naval air units in the amphibious landing at Leyte is an evaluation by two Army Air Force officers who observed the operation.

3. Air Force Evaluation Board, Pacific Ocean Area, "Report Number VI, Evaluation of Conduct and Effectiveness of Air Operations in Pacific Ocean Area Through 15 February 1945." Air Force, 1945. 57 pp.

   This report, based on the situation as it existed on and before 15 February 1945, summarizes the five preceding reports and presents an overall picture and evaluation of the air war in the Pacific Ocean Area.

4.   Air Force Service Command, "Support of Operation Overlord." Air Force, 1944. 57 pp.

   This is a discussion of the planning and participation of the 9th Air Force Service Command in the Normandy invasion.

5.   Air Intelligence Group, Office of the Chief of Naval Operations, "Air War Against Japan, April 1944 to August 1945." DCNO (Air), 1945. 200 pp.

   This series consists of bi-monthly intelligence summaries published during the period indicated.

6.   Airships, Atlantic, "Report on Airship Rescue Operations." Type Commands, 1945. 81 pp. Illustrations.

   This history, illustrated with many excellent and dramatic photographs of LTA rescue operations, contains chronological listings of rescue operations for World War II in the Atlantic and Pacific.

7.   Air, South Pacific, "Administrative History of Commander Aircraft South Pacific." Type Commands, n.d. 173 pp. Table of contents.

   This account is an administrative history of the command. In addition to dealing with aircraft, the history gives an account of the establishment of advance airfields as Japan retreated toward the home islands during the closing years of the war.

8.   ALABAMA (BB-60), Aviation Unit, "History of Aviation Unit, ALABAMA, From Commissioning to 1 January, 1945." Ships, 1945. 19 pp. Appendices.

This is a short history of the battleship's spotting, scouting, and air rescue unit. Most of the account discusses general features of such units and operations in the Gilbert Islands, Kwajalein, Truk, Marianas, Saipan, Philippine Sea, Okinawa, and Luzon campaigns.

9.   ALASKA (CB-1) Aviation Unit, "History of Aviation Unit, ALASKA (CB-1)." Ships, 1945. 10 pp.

This is a short unit history, covering the period February 1944 - May 1945. Operations included Iwo Jima, the Honshu raid, and Third Fleet strikes against Japan.

10.   Alaskan Defense Command, U.S., G-2, "Action on Attu." Army, July 1943. 102 pp. Maps, illustrations.

This account is a detailed summary of Japanese tactics, reactions, weapons, and installations on Attu in the Aleutian Islands. The information was obtained during the operations of the U.S. Northern Force on Attu against the Japanese Occupation Force from 11 May 1943 through mid-July 1943.

11.   Alaskan Defense Command, U.S., G-2, "The Enemy on Kiska." Army, 1943. 102 pp. Maps, illustrations.

This is a detailed report of the information gained about the Japanese as a result of the occupation of Kiska by United Nations troops on 15 August 1943.

12.   Alden, C. S., CAPT, "Brief History of the Naval Transportation Service since June 1937." Individual Personnel, 2 January 1943. 10 pp.

A personal account of the Naval Transportation Service from June 1937 to late 1942 based on Captain Alden's recollections. The author states: "I have not gone into details and explored the files to determine exact dates, but have recorded my observations from memory."

13.   Amerson, A. Binion, Jr., "French Frigate Shoals, A History: 1786 - 1969." Individual Personnel, 1969. 286 pp. Appendices, maps, illustrations.

This is a chronicle of an Hawaiian Atoll that was the site of a Naval Air Station during World War II and is presently the home of a Coast Guard Loran Station. The work is well documented and discusses activities of the Atoll in great detail. One of the appendices contains a list of the Commanding Officers of the Loran Station.

14.   Amphibious Group 5, "The History of Amphibious Group Five, June 1944 to August 1945." Type Commands, n.d. 70 pp. Appendices, maps.

   This chronological narrative summarizes the unit's operations in the Pacific and contains a detailed study of the organization of subordinate components and units. Amphibious Group Five operated at Guam, Saipan, Okinawa, Peleliu, Manus, Guadalcanal, and the Philippines.

15.   Amphibious Group 7, "Command History of Amphibious Group Seven." Type Commands, n.d. 36 pp.

   This history covers the period 21 September 1944 to 14 August 1945 during which the unit carried out operations in the Western Pacific including the Philippines and Okinawa campaigns. A brief chronological narrative is given, as well as the staff organization.

16.   Amphibious Group 11, "Command History of Amphibious Group Eleven." Type Commands, n.d. 8 pp.

   This account covers the operations of the unit from mid-1944 to the end of the war. Among these were the landings in Okinawa and the Philippines. The brief chronological narrative is followed by a description of the staff organization.

17.   Amphibious Group 12, "Command History - Amphibious Group Twelve." Type Commands, 1945. 15 pp.

   This history covers the period from October 1944 to the end of the war in the Pacific. The account gives information on the unit's participation in operations, particularly Okinawa, as well as a description of the staff organization.

18.   Amphibious Group 13, "Command History: Amphibious Group Thirteen." Type Commands, 1945. 18 pp.

   This brief account covers the period January through August 1945. This unit participated in the early stages of preparations for the Okinawa landings before being recalled to Pearl Harbor.

19.   Amphibious Group 14, "Command History: Staff of Commander Amphibious Group Fourteen." Type Commands, n.d. 11 pp.

   This brief account concerns an amphibious group organized in late April, 1945 for a possible invasion of Japan. It is a short study concentrating on training and planning.

20.   AMSTERDAM (CL-101), Aviation Unit, "History of Aviation Unit, AMSTERDAM (CL-101)." Ships, 7 June 1945. 5 pp.

   This is a short unit history regarding training and operations in the United States and Guantanamo Bay, Cuba.

21.   Annapolis, Maryland, Supervisor of Shipbuilding, "Wartime History-Office of Supervisor of Shipbuilding, USN, Annapolis, Maryland." Shore Establishment, 15 January 1946. 20 pp. Appendices.

   This history summarizes in a short narrative the supervisor's wartime activities which related primarily to overseeing the construction of P.T. boats. Organization and administration are gone into in some detail, as well as production control and costs.

22.   Awtrey, H.R., LT, "The Work of the Foreign Section of the Committee on Public Information During the World War: A Tentative Study of the Official Records of the Office of the General Director." Secretary of the Navy, 1941. 79 pp.

   This paper deals with the foreign section of the Creel Committee, which was responsible for devising and administering information programs defending American participation in World War I.

23.   Armed Forces Staff College, "Ryukyus Operation." Type Commands, 1948. 69 pp. Maps, appendices.

   This recounting of the Ryukyus campaign is useful in placing the Okinawa phase within a larger framework. It contains a helpful chronological section and much organizational and unit component data.

24. Army Engineer Corps, "Strategic Engineering Study No. 31: The Island of Sicily, Beaches of Sicily." 2 vols., Army, January 1943. 152 pp. Maps, illustrations.

   This extensive, strategic engineering study of landing beaches of Sicily in preparation for the forthcoming invasion contains excellent maps and photographs.

25. Army Engineer Corps, "Strategic Engineering Study No. 50: Terrain Intelligence, Sicily." Army, January 1943. 56 pp. Maps.

   This extensive, strategic engineering study of the land features of Sicily, in preparation for the forthcoming invasion, contains excellent maps.

26. Army Forces, Central Pacific Area, "Marshall Islands: Japanese Defenses and Battle Damage." Army, March 1944. 58 pp. Appendices, maps, illustrations.

   This report on the defenses used by the Japanese, and the damage to those defenses by U. S. forces in operations on Kwajalein and Eniwetok, is based upon data collected in the field during and immediately after these operations. Direct observation, interviews, photographs, and sketches are the primary sources of the data. Appendix "C" contains 126 photographs. The work also contains references to Tarawa in the Gilberts Islands.

27.   Army Forces, China, Burma, and India, "Final Report, First Special Aviation Project." Army, June 1942. 342 pp. Maps, illustrations.

   This is the final field report of the Halsey-Doolittle Air Raid on Japan. The report has three main divisions: a summation of the entire action; the indexed reports of crewmen and other concerned personnel; and a recommended news release on the operation. Parts I and II analyze the achievements and shortcomings of this joint Army-Navy venture. Part II is very thorough and well documented and comprises the bulk of the report. This draft is in rough form.

28.   Army Forces, Middle Pacific, "History of Army Port and Service Command." Army, 1947. 186 pp. Maps, illustrations.

   This command history covering the period from August 1943 through June 1946 contains a detailed listing of personnel and facilities.

29.   Arnheiter, Marcus A., LCDR, "The Navy in San Francisco Bay: A Current History of Yerba Buena and Treasure Islands." Individual Personnel, 24 July 1968. 169 pp. Appendices, illustrations.

   Collection of anecdotes, folklore, and historical incidents about the islands. The work contains some historical documents as appendices.

30. ASTORIA (CL-90) Aviation Unit, "History of Aviation Unit, ASTORIA (CL-90)." Ships, 1945. 31 pp. Appendices, index.

   This unusually full account of a cruiser's scouting, spotting, and rescue seaplanes gives many accounts of action and covers the period from February 1944 to the war's end. Air operations were conducted in the Philippines, Iwo Jima, and the Japanese mainland.

31. Astoria, Oregon, Combat Information Center Team Training Center, "Command History: March 1944 to April 1945." Admin. Hist. Appen. 21 (16), n.d. 15 pp.

   A particularly well documented account of the origins and activities of a small command quickly organized to fulfill training needs of the wartime fleet.

32. Atlantic Fleet, "Annual Report, FY 1941." Fleets, 1941. 12 pp. Annexes.

   Operations, administration, material readiness, repairs and overhaul, advanced bases, and logistics are discussed.

33. Atlantic Squadron, "Annual Report of Commander Atlantic Squadron, FY 1940." Discontinued Commands, 1940. 34 pp.

   Organization and operations of the Atlantic Squadron are discussed.

34.   Austria, U.S. Forces, Naval Division, "Administrative History, Naval Division, U.S. Element Allied Commission, Austria." Naval Forces, n.d. 16 pp.

   This brief account is a narrative of naval elements assigned to supervise the planning as regards post-World War II Austria. The period covered includes late 1944 through 1 May 1946. The narrative was prepared at the direction of Commander, Naval Forces Europe.

35.   Aviation History Unit, Office of the Chief of Naval Operations, "Inter-Service Cooperation in Aeronautics." CNO, 1948. 58 pp.

   This is a documented historical treatment of Army-Navy cooperation in various aviation projects from 1898 through the end of World War II.

36.   Aviation History Unit, Office of the Chief of Naval Operations, "Progress of Naval Aviation." CNO, 1948. 33 pp.

   This brief account of the history of naval aviation from its origins through 1947 especially covers the 1930s and the post World War II period to 1947.

37.   Azores Naval Forces, "Establishing U.S. Naval Forces In the Azores, January to August 1944." Naval Forces, 1944. 20 pp. Illustrations.

   This is a report from the Commander, U.S. Naval Forces Azores, to Command-In-Chief, U.S. Fleet, on the establishment of a naval base in the Azores. Excellent photographs add to the report.

B

38.   Bahia, Naval Operating Facility, Brazil, "History of U.S. Naval Operating Facility, Bahia, Brazil." Admin. Hist. Appen. 24 (20), n.d. 4 pp. Illustration.

   Briefly traces the facility's history after its establishment on October 1, 1941 to mid-1945.

39.   Baltimore, Maryland, Assistant Industrial Manager, "Brief Official War History of Assistant to the Industrial Manager, Baltimore." Shore Establishment, 20 December 1945. 25 pp. Tables.

   The narrative section of this history is brief, but the tables, which make up the bulk of the account, are comprehensive. The primary function of the installation was ship repair and conversion.

40. Barberton, Ohio, Inspector of Machinery, "Wartime History of Inspection of Naval Machinery, Babcock and Wilcox Company, Barberton, Ohio." Shore Establishment, 1946. 13 pp. Tables.

   This is a general account of an organization developed to inspect the production of naval boilers.

41. Base Force, U.S. Pacific Fleet, "Annual Report of the Commander Base Force, FY 1941." Discontinued Commands, 1941. 35 pp.

   A discussion of organization and training matters for the Base Force, which was a predecessor to the Service Force, Pacific Fleet.

42. Bath, Maine, Supervisor of Shipbuilding, "Wartime History." Shore Establishment, 8 January 1946. 7 pp.

   This is a general history of the activities of this office in inspecting naval shipbuilding and the manufacture of other naval material.

43. Battle Force, U.S. Pacific Fleet, "Annual Report of Commander Battle Force, FY 1941." Discontinued Commands, 1941. 45 pp.

   Operational and readiness matters are discussed.

44.   Bay City and Detroit, Michigan, Supervisor of Shipbuilding, "Wartime History of the Office of the Supervisor of Shipbuilding, USN, Bay City, Michigan, and the Supervisor of Shipbuilding, USN, Detroit, Michigan." Shore Establishment, 27 May 1946. 70 pp.

   This history is a comprehensive presentation of the duties and activities of the Supervisor of Shipbuilding plus such subordinate commands as ship commissioning details. The various contracts awarded also are discussed.

45.   BECUNA (SS-319), "Ship's History of U.S.S. BECUNA (SS-319)." Ships, 15 October 1954. 4 pp.

   A brief account of the patrols of this submarine during 1944-1945 in the Caroline Islands and Leyte Gulf.

46.   Beers, Henry P., "American Naval Occupation and Government of Guam, 1898 - 1902." Administrative Reference Service Report No. 6, Washington: Department of Navy, March 1944. 76 pp. Illustrations.

   This report is an extended analysis of the events on Guam between 1898 and 1902. Described in detail are the capture of the island in June 1898 by a force commanded by Captain Henry Glass, the establishment of U.S. government rule, the administrations of Governors Leary and Schroeder, the history and geography of Guam, and the U.S. Naval activities established in Guam. An excellent bibliography is included.

47.   Beers, Henry P., "The Development of the Office of the Chief of Naval Operations." Individual Personnel, n.d. 119 pp.

   A thorough and well documented study of the office of CNO through the beginning of World War II. This history was published in <u>Military Affairs</u> during 1946-1947.

48.   Beers, Henry P., "U.S. Naval Port Officers in the Bordeaux Region 1917 - 1919." Administrative Reference Service Report No. 3, Washington: Department of the Navy, September 1943. 59 pp. Maps.

   The study describes the conditions at western French ports which handled a constant stream of traffic with the U.S. The duties and responsibilities of the Navy Port Officer and his staff are detailed. Report 3A contains the U.S. Naval Port Regulations of the port of Bordeaux. The author has included an excellent bibliography.

49.   Belem, Brazil, Naval Air Facility, "History of Navy 118." Admin. Hist. Appen. 24 (23), n.d. 9 pp. Maps.

   An outline history of the Naval Air Facility at Belem, Brazil. Covers 19 June 1943 to April 1945.

50.   Belem, Brazil, Naval Operating Facility, "History of Naval Operating Facility Belem, Brazil." Admin. Hist. Appen. 24 (22), n.d. 36 pp. Appendices, charts.

   This is a brief outline history and description of operational functions that covers late 1941 to mid-1945.

51.   Bellinger, Patrick N. L., VADM, "The Gooney Bird." Individual Personnel, circa 1960. 387 pp. Appendices.

   These personal reminiscences cover a broad span of the history of naval aviation from 1912 through 1947. They are in rough draft form. The author was a pioneer in many aspects of aviation.

52.   Beloit, Wisconsin, Inspector of Machinery, "Wartime History of Inspector of Machinery, USN, Beloit, Wisconsin." Shore Establishment, 31 January 1946. 6 pp.

   This account of the inspection of main propulsion machinery and auxiliary diesel generator sets manufactured by Fairbanks, Morse and Company of Beloit, Wisconsin, includes information on production and cost levels. Covering the period 1941-1945, the narrative includes figures on the numbers of people assigned to the facility.

53.   BLUEFISH (SS-222), "History of BLUEFISH (SS-222)." Ships, 25 October 1945. 9 pp. Appendices.

   This is a straight-forward history of a submarine which sank or damaged over 150,000 tons of shipping in the Pacific Theater. Supplemental records name commanding officers and award winners.

54.   Bogota, Colombia, Naval Attache, "An Outline History of Aviation Activities of the Naval Attache', Bogota, Colombia." Shore Establishment, 22 January 1946. 4 pp.

   This is a very brief history of the unit.

55.   Bora Bora, Society Islands, Naval Station, "History of United States Naval Station, Bora Bora, Society Islands of French Oceania." Shore Establishment, 9 July 1945. 230 pp. Appendices, maps, charts.

   Begins with the authorization by the Free French government for U.S. use in early 1942 and concludes with the activities of the Naval Station through mid-1945. It is broad in scope, well organized, and supported by appended data.

56.   Boud, Henry W., LCDR, "Short History of the NOA (APD 24)." Individual Personnel, n.d. 8 pp.

   This is a brief history by a ship's officer. The ship saw action at New Britain, New Guinea, Saipan, Hollandia, and Guam.

57.   Brown, Robert V., LCDR, "The Navy's Mark 15 (Norden) Bomb Sight: Its development and procurement, 1920 - 1945." Individual Personnel, April 1946. 321 pp. Appendices.

   This is a thorough and well-documented history based upon files of the Bureau of Ordnance. The appendices contain a complete list of documents pertaining to the bomb sight.

58.   Brunswick, Maine, Naval Training School, Bowdoin College, "History of Naval Training School, Pre-Radar, Bowdoin College, Brunswick, Maine, April 1941 - November 1945." Admin. Hist. Appen. 30 (2), n.d. 21 pp.

   A condensed, factual account showing the development of a student-officer training program in radar, loran, and radio communications.

59.   Burke, Arleigh A., ADM, "An Evening with Admiral Burke." Individual Personnel, 8 March 1968. 43 pp.

   This discussion between the Admiral and Professor Langdon of the U.S. Naval Academy explores World War II topics and Admiral Burke's tour as CNO.

60. Butler, John A., LT COL, USMC, "Historical Sketch of Office of Naval Attache, Embassy, Ciudad Trujillo, D.R." Shore Establishment, 19 December 1943. 6 pp.

    Lieutenant Colonel Butler served as Naval Attache to Ciudad Trujillo during World War II. His sketch provides a brief discussion of the Dominican Republic political scene during World War II as well as the work of the attache's office. A chronology of important events is included.

C

61. CALIFORNIA (BB-44), Aviation Unit, "History of CALIFORNIA, Aviation Unit." Ships, 3 July 1945, 15 pp. Appendix.

    A short, well-organized and documented unit history, covering the period October 1943 - September 1945, that includes biographies of officers and summaries of flight time for all members of the unit.

62.	Callahan, Arthur E., LT, "History of Commander Naval Bases, South Solomons Sub-Area." Shore Establishment, 1945. 231 pp. Appendices, maps, index.

   Lieutenant Callahan's history is a topically arranged administrative history of this command. Topics covered include an explanation of the command's assigned duty, an examination of command relations, and a review of the command's administration and operations.

63.	Carmichael, George K., CAPT, "The Strategic Employment of Allied Naval Forces in the Pacific During World War II." Individual Personnel, 6 March 1950. 20 pp.

   This is a lecture given at the Naval War College that covers the strategic background and execution of the Pacific war.

64.	Carrier Aircraft Service Units, Fleet Air Wings, Fleet Airship Wings, and Respective Headquarters Squadrons and Supporting Units Ad Hoc Research Group, "Reports." 2 vols., Individual Personnel, 1951. 225 pp.

   This research group, headed by Captain D. F. Smith, undertook extensive investigation of the World War II operations of the indicated units in order to determine eligibility for unit and individual awards. The reports present detailed statistical and outline narrative information on the experiences of these commands. One volume relates to Carrier Aircraft Service Units (CASUs), while the other covers the other commands assigned to this study effort.

65.   Carteret, New Jersey, Assistant Inspector of Machinery, "Wartime History of Office of Assistant Inspector of Machinery, Foster Wheeler Corp., Carteret, N.J." Shore Establishment, 23 February 1946. 9 pp.

This narrative describes the inspection of naval machinery manufactured by the Foster Wheeler Corp. from 9 January 1939 to "V-J" Day in 1945. The firm manufactured boilers, condensers, distillers, expansion joints, and centrifugal pumps. The account stresses evolution of engineering methods. This history makes favorable comments on the role of women as inspectors.

66.   Case, Lynn M., CAPT, USA, "History of AFHQ - Part One: August-December, 1942." Allied Commands, 1945. 1102 pp.

The allied headquarters was the unified inter-allied command in the North African and Mediterranean Theaters. This document is a factual administrative history which limits its scope to the subjects of command administration and organization at the headquarters level during the pre-invasion and invasion periods of the North African Campaign.

67.   Centner, Charles W., Jr., LT, "History of the U.S. Naval Operating Facility, Navy 120." Admin. Hist. Appen. 24 (28), 12 June 1945. 75 pp. Appendices, photographs.

A detailed account of the activities at Recife, Brazil, with extensive documentation. It covers the indications of German influence in Brazil during 1938 that led to the facility's establishment, progress through the war years, and ends in mid-1945, after the order to demobilize had been received.

68.   Central Pacific, Forward Area, "Gunnery Department." Admin. Hist. Appen. 20 (8), n.d. 20 pp.

   An outline of the functions of the supply, stowage, inventory, plans, ground ammunition, ship ammunition, training, towing service, and net and harbor defense sectors of the department.

69.   Central Pacific, Forward Area, "History of Military Government Section." Admin. Hist. Appen. 20 (11), n.d. 2 pp.

   A concise, well written summary of major events. Topics covered are the background to military government activities in the Navy, inception and growth of the section, and its duties.

70.   Central Pacific, Forward Area, "History of Supply Department." Admin. Hist. Appen. 20 (12), n.d. 15 pp.

   A brief chronology and outline with procedures and functions detailed and reasonably well documented.

71.   Central Pacific, Forward Area, "Postal Department." Admin. Hist. Appen. 20 (5), n.d. 7 pp.

   A brief description of postal organization and operations in the Pacific during the final stages of the war.

72.   Central Pacific, Forward Area, "Staff--General." Admin. Hist. Appen. 20 (13), n.d. 16 pp.

   Summaries of the communications, legal, welfare and recreation, chaplain, and educational service departments.

73.   Central Pacific, Forward Area, "Sub-area Commands." Admin. Hist. Appen. 20 (14), n.d. 32 pp.

   A topically organized, well documented overview of the historical evolution of the island and atoll commands in this area during World War II.

74.   Central Pacific, Forward Area, "Utility Air Group." Admin. Hist. Appen. 20 (6), n.d. 5 pp.

   A very brief account of activities from about 1943 to late 1944.

75.   Chaikin, William and Charles H. Coleman, "Shipbuilding Policies of the War Production Board: January 1942 to November 1945." Admin. Hist. Appen. War Admin., 15 April 1947. 207 pp. Appendices.

   This study discusses the War Production Board's role in influencing ship production planning, solving shipbuilding production problems, maintaining production balance, stabilizing the shipyard labor supply, and supervising the modification of older cargo ships.

76.   Challis, George S., LT, "History of the Armed Guard Center (Pacific)." Shore Establishment, 1945. 189 pp. Appendices.

This activity located at Treasure Island, trained and provided guncrews for wartime merchant shipping. Its historical officer presents a solid history of all facets of its establishment and activity. In addition, he offers suggested organizational plans for future Armed Guard Centers.

77.   Chapin, John C., LT, "The Fourth Marine Division in World War II." USMC, August 1945. 53 pp. Appendices, maps, illustrations.

This unit history includes a listing of command and staff personnel and organizational tables, as well as battle accounts. The Fourth Marine Division saw action in such campaigns as Kwajalein, Saipan, Tinian, and Iwo Jima.

78.   Chapin, John C., LT, "The Fifth Marine Division in World War II." USMC, August 1945. 17 pp. Appendices, maps, illustrations.

The appendices of this brief unit history contain a listing of command and staff personnel as well as organizational tables. The Iwo Jima campaign is discussed at some length.

79. CHARLES AUSBURNE (DD-570), "The United States Navy Presents 'A Little Beaver': U.S.S. CHARLES AUSBURNE (DD-570)." Ships, n.d. 6 pp.

   This is a straight-forward command history of the World War II combat operations of a destroyer which at one point was in Admiral Arleigh Burke's squadron.

80. CHICAGO (CA-136), Aviation Unit, "History of the Aviation Unit, U.S.S. CHICAGO (CA-136) from 19 October 1944 - 3 September 1945." Ships, n.d. 24 pp.

   This is a short unit history which discusses the ship's operations with the Third Fleet against Japan.

81. Chicago, Illinois, Supervisor of Shipbuilding, "Wartime History of Supervisor of Shipbuilding, USN, Chicago, Illinois." Shore Establishment, 1946. 33 pp.

   This is a critical review of the principles, practices, and procedures utilized by the Supervisor of Shipbuilding in Chicago from the establishment of that office in early 1941 until January 1946. Comments on governmental-industry cooperation in labor relations and the disposition of surplus material after V-J Day are noteworthy, as is the account of facilities acquisitioned by Pullman-Standard Car Manufacturing Company and Chicago Bridge and Iron Company at war's end. Some information on the value of naval contracts is included.

82.   Chief of Naval Operations, "Annual Report of the Chief of Naval Operations, 1932-1941." CNO, 1932-1941. 343 pp.

   These individual annual reports give overall information and statistics on such matters as construction, fleet readiness, and training.

83.   Cleveland, Ohio, Inspector of Machinery, "Wartime History (1939-1945) - Office of the Inspector of Machinery, USN, Cleveland, Ohio." Shore Establishment, 19 February 1946. 15 pp.

   This account concerns the production and inspection of diesel engines for the Navy at the Cleveland Diesel Engine Division of General Motors Corporation. The emphasis is on departmental functions, but figures on production levels also are included.

84.   Cleveland, Ohio, Supervisor of Shipbuilding, "Office of Supervisor of Shipbuilding, USN, Cleveland, Ohio, Wartime History." Shore Establishment, 1945. 16 pp.

   In addition to a quantitative report on personnel assigned to this office, this account includes data on the nature of the shipbuilding projects supervised. Particular emphasis is given to individual companies and their specific role in war production.

85.   Coast Guard Headquarters, "The Coast Guard at War." 23 vols., Coast Guard, 1948. Maps, illustrations.

A detailed summary of the role of the Coast Guard immediately prior to and during World War II. The Naval History Division possesses volumes I-XXII, and XXX. The work includes many direct quotations from members of the Guard. A version of this history was published by the U.S. Naval Institute in 1957.

86.   Coast Guard, Research and Statistics Section, Operations Division, "The Accomplishments of Ten Coast Guard Cutters Transferred to The United Kingdom." Coast Guard, 1942. 37 pp. Appendices, illustrations.

A thorough description and history of ten 250-foot cutters prior to their transfer to the United Kingdom in April 1941. The study also describes the manner in which the transfer was effected. The appendices contain records of movement of each ship and cost data.

87.   Coast Guard, Research and Statistical Section, Operations Division, "Bering Sea Patrol." Coast Guard, 1942. 80 pp. Appendices, maps, illustrations.

A thorough discussion of the legal foundations and operations of the Bering Sea Patrol from its inception as a seal protection patrol in 1912 through its more complex defense role at the end of 1941. Appendices contain the executive orders and acts of Congress relating to the patrol. Several case studies are in the body of the text.

88.   Coast Guard, Research and Statistics Section, Operations Division, "Greenland." Coast Guard, 1943. 49 pp. Maps, illustrations.

This study discusses the demographic and topographic features of Greenland and traces the history of the U.S.-Denmark agreement providing for the defense of Greenland. The final pages are a brief discussion of Coast Guard operations in the Greenland area in 1941-42.

89.   Coast Guard, Research and Statistics Section, Operations Division, "The Taking of Italian, German and Danish Merchant Vessels in Ports of The United States in Protective Custody By The United States Coast Guard." Coast Guard, 1942. 52 pp. Appendices, maps, illustrations.

This discusses the legal justification and immediate events preceding the taking into custody of the ships on March 30, 1941. The appendices contain a listing and descriptions of the ships. Photographs of the larger ships are included.

90.   Cohn, David L., "The Battle of Makassar Straits." Individual Personnel, n.d. 16 pp.

Mr. Cohn's article describes the battle of 23-24 January 1942 in which four American destroyers surprised a Japanese Transport Squadron off Borneo and sank numerous enemy vessels before withdrawing intact. According to marginal notations the story was related to the author by Admiral William A. Glassford, Jr., who commanded the task force. The draft was intended as a magazine article.

91. Coleman, Charles H., "Shipbuilding Activities of the National Defense Advisory Commission and Office of Production Management: July 1940 to December 1941." Admin. Hist. Appen. War Admin., 5 April 1946. 148 pp. Appendices.

   This study relates the Commission's administration of the separate shipbuilding programs of the Navy and the Maritime Commission, whose needs had to be met by many of the same shipyard facilities. It is primarily concerned with explaining the role of governmental coordination.

92. CONCORD (CL-10), Aviation Unit, "History of the U.S.S. CONCORD Aviation Scouting Unit." Ships, May 1945. 6 pp. Appendices.

   This short unit history covers the period from 7 December 1941 to 1 September 1945. CONCORD (CL-10) operated in the North Pacific and saw little enemy action.

93. Condit, Kenneth, Gerald Diamond, and Edwin Turnbladh, "U.S. Marine Corps. Ground Training in World War II." U.S.M.C., 1956. 353 pp.

   This is a thorough and well documented study of procurement and training of Marines from 8 September 1939 to 14 August 1945. A ten page bibliography provides a valuable guide for additional research.

94.   Conolly, Richard L., ADM, "The Landing at Salerno In World War II." Individual Personnel, 14 May 1957. 10 pp.

   This is a copy of an address delivered to the Naval Historical Foundation by the task force commander in the Salerno Operation. It provides not only a battle narrative, but also the Admiral's views on the tactical and strategic considerations of the invasion.

95.   Construction Battalion 53, "United States Naval Construction Battalion 53." Shore Establishment, n.d. 10 pp.

   Construction Battalion 53 participated in the invasions of Bougainville and Guam and the construction of the Atomic Test Site at Bikini. This brief history includes a chronology and photographs.

96.   Construction Battalion 71, "History of The Seventy-First U.S. Naval Construction Battalion." Shore Establishment, n.d. 24 pp.

   Although undocumented the history provides a thorough and detailed account of the achievements of Construction Battalion 71, which participated in the invasions of Bougainville and Okinawa.

97.   Construction Battalion 74, "United States Naval Construction Battalion 74." Shore Establishment, n.d. 5 pp.

   The brief narrative treats highlights which included the Tarawa and Marshalls operations.

98.   Construction Battalion Maintenance Unit 520, "Historical Narrative--CBMU 520." Admin. Hist. Appen. 34 (15)(A), 12 June 1945. 49 pp. Photographs.

The operations from February 1944 through June 1945 on Guadalcanal of this unit are covered.

99.   Construction Battalion Maintenance Unit 533, "The History of U.S. Naval Construction Battalion Maintenance Unit No. 533." Admin. Hist. Appen. 34 (15)(A), n.d. 66 pp. Photographs.

This history begins with the commissioning of CBMU 533 in September 1943 and covers pre-mobilization training and the unit's deployment to Guadalcanal in early 1944.

100.   Construction Battalion Maintenance Unit 537, "Historical Narrative of U.S. Naval Construction Battalion Maintenance Unit 537." Admin. Hist. Appen. 34 (15)(A), 1 July 1945. 8 pp.

A brief, clearly written narrative of the major events in the history of a unit whose function was to maintain and operate advanced bases in the vicinity of New Caledonia. Also included with this history is a scrapbook with numerous photographs of unit personnel.

101.   Construction Battalion Maintenance Unit 550, "Organization and Operation of U.S. Naval Construction Battalion Maintenance Unit 550." Admin. Hist. Appen. 34 (15)(A), 15 August 1944. 22 pp.

The officer-in-charge's appraisal of his unit's activities, training, operations, and problems while serving on Guadalcanal.

102.   Construction Brigade, Third Naval, "History of the Third United States Naval Construction Brigade In The Second World War." Shore Establishment, n.d. 17 pp. Appendices, illustrations.

The Third Construction Brigade comprised all Seventh Fleet Construction Forces in the Southwest Pacific Area in 1944 and 1945. This undocumented history provides a general summary of the Brigade's activities. Photographs and tables outlining the disposition of forces are included.

103.   Construction Troops, Task Unit 55.1.3, "History of Naval Construction Troops Task Unit 55.1.3 on Okinawa." Admin. Hist. Appen. 38 (29), October 1945. 68 pp. Photographs.

This report provides a close-up account of the damage and rebuilding following the typhoon of October 9, 1945.

104.		Corson, Robert W., LTJG, "Wartime History of The United States Naval Ammunition Depot, Hingham, Mass." Shore Establishment, 1945. 77 pp. Illustrations.

Lieutenant Corson's history of the Hingham Ammunition Depot primarily discusses the administration of the depot, dwelling on the expansion of personnel and facilities necessitated by the war. A brief pre-war history of the depot is included. No bibliographical documentation is provided, although photographs are extensive.

D

105.		Dansville, New York, Assistant Inspector of Machinery, "Wartime History of the Office of the Assistant Inspector of Machinery, Foster Wheeler Corporation, Dansville, New York." Shore Establishment, 1946. 3 pp.

Primarily a statement of the duties of the Assistant Inspector and the situations he encountered.

106.   Danver, James A., "Early History of Motor Torpedo Boat Squadron Thirteen." Type Commands, n.d. 125 pp.

   This personal account covers the initial training activities of the squadron at New Orleans and continues through the campaign in the Aleutians during the winter of 1943-1944. The author served as Executive Officer in the Squadron.

107.   Dashiell, G. W. D., CAPT, "History of the Port Director (NTS), San Pedro, California." Shore Establishment, 20 September 1945. 38 pp.

   Captain Dashiell's account covers the period he was Port Director from September 1940 to October 1945. The greater part of the narrative discusses administrative functions and responsibilities rather than operations.

108.   Davis, Robert G., CAPT (MC), "Canacao Journal." Individual Personnel, 3 June 1946. 149 pp. Appendices.

   This is the official journal of the United States Naval Hospital, Canacao, Philippine Islands, from 5 November 1941 to 9 May 1942. It is an interesting historical account of the functioning of the hospital during the Japanese occupation of the Philippines.

109.   Davis, Vernon E., "The History of the Joint Chiefs of Staff in World War II: Organizational Development." 2 vols., Joint Chiefs of Staff, 1953. 812 pp.

   Vol. I: "Origin of the Joint and Combined Chiefs of Staff." This volume traces the institutional development of the JCS beginning with the Joint Army and Navy Board in 1903. Cooperation with the British in pre-war planning and strategic decision-making after Pearl Harbor played a significant role in the evolution of the JCS, which was modeled in part on British principles. The story is carried through the spring of 1942 to illustrate the initial period of orientation and adjustment.

   Vol. II: "Development of the JCS Committee Structure." This volume deals in detail with the various components of the JCS organization. Of particular importance is the major committee reorganization of May 1943.

110.   Dean, John M., Jr., LT, "History of Group One, Fleet Air Wing Seventeen." Type Commands, n.d. 81 pp.

   This history covers the period from January to August 1945 and relates the missions by Group One, Fleet Air Wing Seventeen stationed on Mindoro in the Philippines. The unit engaged in patrol activities west of the islands and over those parts of Southeast Asia controlled by the Japanese. The work concentrates on the accomplishments of individual units and flyers.

111.   Demolition Units, Atlantic, "Demolition Units of the Atlantic Theater of Operations." Shore Establishment, n.d. 9 pp.

    A brief history of the training and mission of naval demolition units participating in the Normandy landing.

112.   Destroyer Squadron Fifty-Six, "Combat Record of Destroyer Squadron Fifty-Six." Type Commands, 1945. 12 pp.

    This brief history deals primarily with the squadron's operations during the latter part of 1944 and all of 1945 at Lingayen and Leyte Gulf. A summary of each vessel's activities during the period is recorded.

113.   Destroyers, Pacific Fleet, "History of the Anti-Submarine Warfare Training Center." Admin. Hist. Appen. 38 (14)(A), 10 September 1945. 73 pp. Appendices, charts.

    This study consists mainly of a chronology, supported by charts and photographs, of the development of the ASW Training Center at Pearl Harbor.

114.   Detroit and Bay City, Michigan, Supervisor of Shipbuilding, "Wartime History of the Supervisor of Shipbuilding, Detroit and Bay City, Michigan." Shore Establishment, 20 March 1946. 42 pp.

    This account is a narrative of the shipbuilding facilities and contracts supervised by this activity and related costs, inspections and administration.

115.   Dingwell, John E., CAPT, "Planning Naval Advanced Bases." Individual Personnel, n.d. 72 pp.

   This narrative outlines the planning and development required to establish advanced naval bases, from their basic concept in the Navy Department to their operational phases.

116.   Director of Flight, Office of the Chief of Naval Operations, "Administrative History of Naval Aviation." CNO, 23 October 1944. 180 pp. Appendices, charts.

   This history is composed of several subordinate sectional summaries of operations, aerology, flight statistics, and medical liaison, which primarily cover the period 1921 to 1944. In addition, a resume of significant events in naval aviation from 1917 to 1927 is included. The primary focus of the document is administrative rather than operational.

117.   District, First Naval, "First Naval District History--Aviation." Admin. Hist. Appen. 15 (TT), n.d. 220 pp. Appendices.

   This comprehensive history of naval aviation in the First Naval District during the late 1930's and early 1940's contains sections on facilities, auxiliary air stations, and major air stations within the district.

118. District, First Naval, "History of the Dartmouth College V-12 Unit: 1943 - 1945." Admin. Hist. Appen. 15 (QQ), n.d. 82 pp. Appendices.

   A thorough and detailed history of one of the prototype NROTC units. The study is reasonably well annotated and the format comprehensive. Appendices contribute to the understanding of the early officer-training processes in a collegiate setting.

119. District, First Naval, "History of Harbor Entrance Control Post Boston." Admin. Hist. Appen. 15 (VV), n.d. 70 pp. Appendices, charts.

   During its period of service, 4 August 1941 to 27 June 1945, the role of the control post changed from ship movement observation to control of all ship movements through the harbor entrance. The brief narrative is supported by extensive appended data.

120. District, Third Naval, "Historical Narrative of Assistant Commandant (Logistics), Third Naval District." Admin. Hist. Appen. 23 (2), 28 June 1945. 178 pp. Appendices.

   A brief summary covers the period from 2 November 1943 to 1 January 1945, while the balance of the document is composed of appendices.

121.   District, Third Naval, "Historical Narrative of the District Communications Office, 3ND." Admin. Hist. Appen. 23 (3), 8 October 1945. 100 pp. Appendices, charts.

The lengthy but well-written document covers the period 8 September 1939 to 14 August 1945.

122.   District, Third Naval, "Historical Narrative of District Intelligence Office, 3ND." Admin. Hist. Appen. 23 (4)(A), 30 October 1945. 195 pp. Appendices, charts, photographs.

This detailed account of the activities of the Intelligence Office from 1 September 1939 to 14 August 1945 provides insight into counter-espionage and counter-sabotage operations, and contains information on files kept on Japanese prior to the outbreak of hostilities.

123.   District, Third Naval, "Historical Narrative of the District Material Office (October 13, 1939 - April 30, 1942) and Field Production Division, Navy Yard, New York (May 1, 1942 - December 31, 1945)." Naval Districts, 1945. 381 pp. Appendices, maps, illustrations.

This account describes building and repair activities in private shipyards in the New York City area. A history of degaussing, magnetic compass, and anti-torpedo device activities of the New York Navy Yard is included.

124.   District, Third Naval, "Historical Narrative of District Security Office, Third Naval District." Admin. Hist. Appen. 23 (I), 19 September 1945. 35 pp.

    This well organized, carefully written report covers the period 13 October 1941 to 14 August 1945.

125.   District, Third Naval, "History of the Office of the Inspector of Naval Material, Buffalo, New York, September 1939 - July 1945." Shore Establishment, 19 November 1945. 50 pp. Appendices.

    This administrative history provides an excellent, well-documented examination of administrative problems involved in the procurement of war materials in Western New York during World War II. Topics include problems associated with converting industry to a war footing, mounting production requirements from 1939 to 1945, and administrative and organizational developments necessitated by these requirements. The text is supplemented with statistical appendices.

126.   District, Third Naval, "Port Director Third Naval District Historical Report." Admin. Hist. Appen. 23 (5), 13 April 1945. 44 pp.

    The well-written document relies on example rather than comprehensive detail to describe the operations of the port of New York from 1 July 1944 to 31 December 1944.

127.   District, Fourth Naval, "History of the Fourth Naval District, Part XIV, History of the U.S. Naval Ammunition Depot, Fort Miflin." Admin. Hist. Appen. 45 (4), n.d. 39 pp. Photographs.

    This report begins with an historical resume of the uses of this site from colonial days to the present. Administration, production, maintenance, and military organization during World War II are covered in subsequent chapters.

128.   District, Fifth Naval, Office of the Director of Distribution, "History of the Office of Director of Distribution, Fifth Naval District, N.O.B., Norfolk, Virginia." Admin. Hist. Appen. 42 (1), n.d. 65 pp. Charts, photographs.

    This document surveys the activities of the Fifth Naval District Personnel Office from 1939 through 1945. The administrative problems related to the influx of personnel during the war are stressed.

129.   District, Fifth Naval, "War Record of the Fifth Naval District, 1942." Naval Districts, 1943. 461 pp. Charts, photographs, appendices.

    This history deals with the attacks of German submarines on allied shipping and the countermeasures taken by combined U.S. units operating out of the 5th Naval District. Charts detailing German submarine movement are provided, along with various photographs.

130.   District, Seventh Naval, Industrial Manager, "Wartime History of The Industrial Manager, Seventh Naval District." Shore Establishment, 8 August 1945. 30 pp.

　　　This history is a series of interrelated graphs, charts, and tables showing the tasks accomplished by the unit from 1 May 1942 to 1 May 1945. The organization was concerned with ship conversion and construction in the Miami, Florida area.

131.   District, Twelfth Naval, "History of District Intelligence Office, Twelfth Naval District." Naval Districts, 1946. 81 pp.

　　　This interesting account covers the period 1921-1945. It illustrates the type of intelligence effort on the West Coast prior to and during World War II.

132.   District, Fourteenth Naval, "A Brief Study of Pearl Harbor in its Relation to the U.S. Navy." Shore Establishment, 1933. 121 pp.

　　　The narrative contains sections dealing with the historical development of the American naval facility on Oahu; a resume of appropriations, 1898-1930; a history of channel and harbor development at Pearl Harbor; a monograph on the mooring mast and lighter-than-air station; and a history of Medical Department activities in the 14th Naval District.

133.	District, Fourteenth Naval, Office of the Director of Training, "History of the Fourteenth Naval District, Director of Training Office." Admin. Hist. Appen. 43 (3), n.d. 55 pp.

A detailed assessment of the coordinating responsibilities of the Director of Training with a brief history of each of the seven specialized sections under his supervision.

134.	District, Fifteenth Naval, Marine Officer, "Report of Activities and Duties Performed by the Second and Third Guard Companies, Marine Barracks, Naval Operating Base, Balboa, Canal Zone." Shore Establishment, 11 March 1946. 13 pp.

This brief recounting of the World War II period contains the original war diary of the companies.

135.	Douglas, L. H., LT, "Submarine Disarmament in the Interwar Period." Individual Personnel, 14 June 1968. 19 pp. Appendices.

This is a short summary of the series of international disarmament conferences from 1924-1936 that dealt with the submarine issue. The author presents a useful analysis of the position of each major maritime power. The appendix contains a complete listing of research sources on submarine disarmament in this period.

136.   Dowling, George B., CAPT (MC), "Special Report of United States Naval Medical Service in the Invasion of Normandy." Individual Personnel, 11 January 1945. 31 pp. Appendices, illustrations.

This is a report on the medical services rendered by the medical section of the Western Naval Task Force from 6 June to 10 July 1944. Appendices contain pertinent operation orders and officer reports.

137.   Dulin, Robert O., Jr., Midshipman, "The YAMATO Class - A Design Study." Individual Personnel, 1961. 18 pp. Appendices, illustrations.

This term paper by a Naval Academy midshipman discusses the design, construction, and careers of the battleships of the YAMATO class. The appendices contain technical data.

138.   Duluth, Minnesota, Assistant Supervisor of Shipbuilding, "Wartime History of Assistant Supervisor of Shipbuilding, USN, Duluth, Minnesota Office." Shore Establishment, 6 November 1945. 7 pp.

The narrative deals primarily with administrative procedures and recommendations for future use.

E

139. Eighth Fleet, "The Administrative History of the Eighth Fleet." Fleets, n.d. 100 pp.

    This is an administrative history of the conception, planning, assembling, organization, and training of the amphibious forces which conducted the landings in French Morocco, Sicily, Salerno, Anzio, and Southern France. The account is well documented and well organized.

140. Emergency Shiphandling Training Unit 1, "History of Emergency Shiphandling Training Unit 1." Admin. Hist. Appen. 38 (14)(A), 4 September 1945. 135 pp. Appendices, charts, photographs.

    A four-page summary of this command's development of emergency shiphandling training, in which mechanical simulators were used rather than actual ships. It is supported by extensive appendices.

141. ENTERPRISE (CV-6), "Narrative History and Chronological Order of Events, U.S.S. ENTERPRISE (CV-6) 12 May 1938 - 25 September 1945." Ships, 1 October 1945. 13 pp.

    This wartime history is about the ship Secretary of The Navy Forrestal called the "one vessel that most nearly symbolizes the history of the Navy in this war."

142.   Espiritu Santo, New Hebrides, Naval Air Base, "A History of Naval Aviation at Espiritu Santo." Admin. Hist. Appen. SoPac. Admin. Hist. 6, n.d. 70 pp.

The document thoroughly covers the development of the Navy air base on this Pacific island during World War II.

143.   Espiritu Santo, New Hebrides, Naval Base, Civil Affairs Office, "History of Civil Affairs." Admin. Hist. Appen. SoPac. Admin. Hist. 16, n.d. 28 pp.

The Civil Affairs office was established in June 1943 to serve as a liaison between the local government and the Army and Navy forces occupying the island. This history presents the entire scope of its activities.

144.   Essington, Pennsylvania, Inspector of Machinery, "History of the Office of the Inspector of Machinery, USN, Westinghouse Electric Corporation, Essington, Pennsylvania, During the Period World War I to 1 January 1946." Shore Establishment, 1946. 13 pp.

This account deals with a plant which, during maximum wartime production, employed over 11,500 people in the manufacture of turbines, gears, forced draft blowers, turbogenerators, pumps, and water brakes. Noteworthy in this account are tables summarizing production levels.

145.   Europe Naval Forces, "Administrative History, U.S. Naval Forces in Europe, 1940-1946." 8 parts. Forces, 1946, 1947. 611 pp. Appendices.

This eight-part series covers activities of the Special Naval Observer, London, the Commander U.S. Naval Forces in Europe, and the Commander Twelfth Fleet. The preparation for the Normandy Operation is discussed at length. The historical account is carried through 1 March 1947.

146.   Europe Naval Forces, "Historical Narrative - Staff Medical Office." Forces, 1945. 27 pp.

An overview of the Staff Medical Office which emphasizes the supportive role it played in the Normandy Operation.

147.   Europe Naval Forces, "Historical Narrative: U.S. Naval Components to S.H.A.E.F./U.S.F.E.T. Missions to Liberated Countries in Northwest Europe." Naval Forces, 1946. 15 pp.

These brief narratives deal with U.S. Naval Forces in liberated Belgium, Holland, Denmark, and Norway. The accounts were compiled by the Commander U.S. Naval Forces, Europe.

148.   Europe Naval Forces, "History of the Command of the SUSNLO, Italy and Deputy Chief, Navy Sub-Commission, Allied Commission For Italy." Naval Forces, 1946. 49 pp.

   The history of command of the Senior U. S. Naval Liaison Officer, Italy covers the period 29 September 1943 to 1 November 1945 and concerns itself with a description of the operations of the naval occupation forces and intelligence gathering activities throughout Italy.

149.   Europe Naval Forces, "Office of the United States Naval Attache, American Embassy, London, England, 1939-1946." Shore Establishment, 1946. 90 pp. Illustrations.

   Noteworthy for its extensive documentation and factual detail, this administrative history of the U. S. Naval Attache in London traces the wartime development of the offices of the Naval Attache and the Naval Attache for Air and their relationships with other American and British commands. Particular attention is given to the organizational relationship between the Attache and Commander U. S. Naval Forces in Europe, notably in matters of intelligence gathering.

150.   Europe, Naval Technical Mission, Historical Section, "Office of Naval Operations Technical Mission in Europe." Shore Establishment, 1945. 280 pp. Appendices.

The Naval Technical Mission in Europe was established in 1944 to study and exploit German scientific and technological intelligence which came into Allied hands at the end of the war. This is essentially an administrative history with an appendix listing all reports prepared by the Mission.

151.   Exmouth Gulf, Australia, Advanced Base, "Notes on Exmouth Gulf Advanced Base - World War II Operation 'Potshot'." Shore Establishment, n.d. 4 pp. Appendices.

These notes provide a brief history of this advanced submarine base in Australia.

F

152. Fahrney, Delmer S., RADM, "The History of Pilotless Aircraft and Guided Missiles." Shore Establishment-BUAER, n.d. 1345 pp.

   This 16-chapter work traces the development of U.S. and foreign missile programs up to 1948. Much space is given to pre-war development, particularly on the part of the Navy. Combat use of "missiles" in World War II is described.

153. FALL RIVER (CA-131), Aviation Unit, "History of the U.S.S. FALL RIVER Aviation Unit." Ships, 1 September 1945. 12 pp. Appendices, illustrations.

   This is organized into a chronology, narrative, and appendix. The ship and unit were commissioned on 15 February 1945.

154. Farenholt, Ammen, RADM (MC), "War Record of U.S.S. FARENHOLT (Number 2) (DD-491)." Ships, October 1945. 17 pp.

   The period covered is April 1942 - March 1945. Rear Admiral Farenholt gives a straightforward war-record narrative and summary of operations. There is no documentation, but a related file includes his research notes and typed statements from crew members. FARENHOLT saw much combat in the Pacific Theater.

155. Felt, Harry D., ADM, "An Evening With Admiral Harry D. Felt." Individual Personnel, 4 March 1968. 25 pp.

This is an interview at the U.S. Naval Institute, Annapolis, by Professor Clark Reynolds with the Admiral regarding a range of issues. World War II and the 1958--1964 period, when Admiral Felt was Commander in Chief, Pacific, are emphasized.

156. Fernando do Noronha, Brazil, Naval Air Facility, "History of U.S. Naval Air Facility, Fernando do Noronha, Brazil." Admin. Hist. Appen. 24 (26), n.d. 54 pp. Appendices, photographs.

This narrative covers early 1944 to 30 June 1945.

157. Fifth Marine Division, G-2, "Special Study of the Enemy Situation." USMC, 16 November 1944. 19 pp. Maps, illustrations.

This is a summary of Japanese strength and installations in Nanpo Shoto (or Bonins) in late 1944. Detailed maps are included.

158. Fighting Squadron 6, "The War Record of Fighting Squadron Six, 7 December 1941 - 20 June 1942." Type Commands, 27 March 1963. 67 pp. Illustrations.

This history is in log form and summarizes the daily operations of an aviation unit assigned to ENTERPRISE from the outbreak of war to 20 June 1942. The Battle of Midway is covered in some detail. The work includes pertinent news articles.

159.	Fighting Squadron 23, "Story of 'Fighting Twenty-Three'." Type Commands, n.d. 30 pp.

This history is in the form of a daily chronology from 16 November 1942 to 11 May 1944. This aviation unit participated in most of the major Pacific actions.

160.	First Corps, Sixth Army, "History of the Biak Operation, 15-27 June 1944." Army, 1944. 79 pp. Maps, illustrations.

This well-documented narrative of operations on Biak, on which the Japanese had strong defensive positions, contains orders, instructions, and reports reproduced verbatim. Biak Island is off the coast of Northwest New Guinea. This operation was one of the preliminary steps prior to the 1944 Philippines campaign.

161.	Fitzgerald, Oscar P., "Naval Group China: A Study of Guerrilla Warfare During World War II." Individual Personnel, February 1968. 119 pp. Maps.

A M.A. thesis giving details on the group commanded by Captain Milton E. Miles which advised and trained Nationalist guerrillas. A bibliography includes a listing of unpublished materials.

162.   Flint, Michigan, Naval Training School (Amphibious Engineers), "Administrative History, Naval Training School (Amphibious Engineers), General Motors Institute, Flint, Michigan." Admin. Hist. Appen. 30 (1), 1 August 1945. 11 pp.

The well-organized report describes the general history of the station, its major training programs and the background and methods of the General Motors Training Institute, with a section on general comments and recommendations.

163.   Fortaleza Naval Air Facility, Brazil, "Historical Report." Admin. Hist. Appen. 24 (25), n.d. 40 pp. Appendices, photographs.

The narrative outlines naval air activities at Fortaleza, 15 November 1943 to mid-1945.

164.   Fourth Base Depot, U.S.M.C., Russell Islands, "History of Base Depot, Russell Islands." Admin. Hist. Appen. SoPac. Admin. Hist. 74, n.d. 74 pp.

The narrative covers the organization of the Fourth Base Depot in World War II, its establishment, mission, development, and general operations with a separate record of each supply company and subordinate unit within the command.

165.   Fourth Fleet, "History of Fleet Post Office Recife and District Postal Officer, Fourth Fleet." Admin. Hist. Appen. 24 (4), n.d. 6 pp.

This first-person account of the establishment of mail service for the South Atlantic area was written by the postal officer.

166.   Fourth Fleet, "A History of the South Atlantic Campaign." Fleets, n.d. 245 pp. Appendices.

This history covers both the diplomatic and the military aspects of the Fourth Fleet in the South Atlantic from 1941-1945. Though not footnoted, the account is well organized and has a table of contents. An untitled 64-page supplement accompanies the document. It contains an excellent chronology of events throughout the war in the South Atlantic and carries the story on through the disestablishment of the force.

167.   Fox, Leonard J., CPO, "Pearl Harbor." Individual Personnel, n.d. 5 pp.

This is a brief reminiscence by a Chief Petty Officer on board HELENA as the Japanese attack began.

168.   France Naval Forces, "Historical Narrative of the U.S. Naval Task Group, France." Naval Forces, 1945. 11 pp.

   In this brief work, the emphasis is on the later stages of the Task Group, particularly the withdrawal of its units from various countries.

169.   France Naval Forces, "Historical Narrative: United States Navy in France." Naval Forces, 1946. 65 pp.

   This narrative concerns U.S. Naval activities in France from the establishment of Commander, U.S. Ports and Bases, France (CTF 125) on 10 July 1944 until its dissolution on 1 July 1945. Footnotes are copious. A table of contents and a brief summary are included.

170.   Forthingham, Donald, CAPT, "Historical Narrative-U.S. Naval Component, SHAEF - Mission, Netherlands; U.S. Naval Section, USFET - Mission Netherlands." Naval Forces, 1946. 13 pp.

   The history of missions from the Supreme Headquarters Allied Expeditionary Forces, Europe and U.S. Forces European Theater in the Netherlands covers December 1944 to October 1945. During this period the British and American navies cooperated in civilian relief and in training Dutch Forces, among other activities.

171.   Furer, Julius A., RADM, "History of the Office of the Coordinator of Research and Development From 12 July 1941 to 19 May 1945." Shore Establishment, 1945. 28 pp. Appendices.

During the period of American participation in World War II, Admiral Furer served as the Navy's Coordinator of Research and Development. His history examines the origin and development of scientific research in the Navy, the establishment of his office, its relationship to other offices and agencies, and its internal organization. Particular attention is given to an explanation of the policies and procedures that he developed as coordinator. Appendices include organizational flow charts, biographical sketches of key personnel, and descriptions of major projects undertaken by his office.

G

172.   Gally, Benjamin W., LTCOL, USMC, "A History of U.S. Fleet Landing Exercises." Discontinued Commands, n.d. 14 pp.

This is a brief study of five fleet landing exercises conducted from 1934-1939. Culebra Island, Puerto Rico, was the scene for exercises 1, 2, 4, and 5. The third exercise took place in the San Pedro - San Clemente area.

173.   General Purchasing Agent, European Theater,
Service Forces, "We Bought The Eiffel Tower."
Army, 1 October 1945. 228 pp. Maps, illustrations.

   The story of the office of the General Purchasing Agent in the European Theater from its inception in the spring of 1942 until the end of hostilities in Europe in 1945. The book includes statistics as well as personal anecdotes on the problems confronting the office in coordinating the local procurement of supplies, equipment, and facilities in liberated, occupied, and neutral countries in Europe.

174.   Germany Naval Forces, "Historical Narrative: Commander, U.S. Naval Forces, Germany." Naval Forces, n.d. 78 pp.

   This account covers the dissolution of the German fleet after World War II and the activities of U.S. Naval units in Germany. The work is footnoted, but there is no index or table of contents. Some of the topics covered include personnel, logistics, operations, mission, intelligence, shipping, and the Naval Directorate.

175.   Germany Naval Forces, "History of Task Force 126, United States Ports and Bases, Germany." Naval Forces, 1946. 25 pp.

   This account is primarily an administrative history of Task Force-126 from 15 December 1944 until its dissolution on 10 November 1945. The history especially relates to U.S. port activities at Bremen and Bremerhaven.

176.   Germany Naval Forces, "Office of Naval Advisor, Office of Military Government of Germany." Joint Commands, 1945. 33 pp.

This provides both an administrative and operational account of American Naval forces in Germany and associated planning activities from November 1944 to April 1946. These organizations were charged with such responsibilities as prisoners of war, disarming and demobilizing German armed forces, ocean shipping control, and military intelligence.

177.   Ghormley, Robert L., VADM, "South Pacific Command: Events Leading Up To U.S. Attack on Solomon Islands." Forces, 1943. 23 pp.

This brief narrative was apparently prepared to accompany several motion picture films. It is largely a personal account of Admiral Ghormley's experiences as Commander South Pacific from April - October 1942 until relieved by Admiral Halsey.

178.   Ghormley, Robert L., VADM, "South Pacific Command History: Early Period." Forces, 1943. 150 pp.

A personal account discussing his tour as the South Pacific Commander until relieved by Admiral Halsey in late 1942.

179.	Glenn, Bess, "Demobilization of Civilian Personnel by the U.S. Navy After the First World War." Administrative Reference Service Report No. 8, Washington: Department of Navy, February 1945. 43 pp. Index.

   After a brief introduction on how the U.S. Navy recruited and held employees during World War I, the rest of the study describes the methods and actions taken by the Department of the Navy to reduce its number of civilians after World War I.

180.	Goodman, Warren H., CAPT, USMC, "The First Marine Aircraft Wing." USMC, n.d. 9 pp.

   This is a very brief account of the unit's actions at Guadalcanal, New Georgia, Bougainville, and Rabaul.

181.	Goodman, Warren H., CAPT, USMC, "Marine Corps Aviation In World War II: December 7, 1941 - December 7, 1944." USMC, 1945. 15 pp. Maps.

   This is a brief chronology of some of the outstanding events in the first three years of the air war in the Pacific.

182.	Goodman, Warren H., CAPT, USMC, "The Second Marine Aircraft Wing." USMC, n.d. 11 pp.

   This is a brief account of the unit from July 1941 to December 1944 in such actions as Wake Island, Midway, Guadalcanal, and New Georgia.

183.   Gray, James S., Jr., CAPT, "Decision at Midway." Individual Personnel, n.d. 12 pp.

   This short but valuable account deals with the participation of Fighting Squadron Six in the Battle of Midway as remembered by the unit commander.

184.   GUAM (CB-2), Aviation Unit, "History of The Aviation Unit, U.S.S. GUAM (CB-2)." Ships, 31 May 1945. 6 pp.

   This short unit history, covering the period September 1944 to 30 September 1945, concerns one of the first units to operate the Curtiss Seahawk scout seaplane (SC-1).

H

185.   HALF MOON (AVP-26), "The HALF MOON Views Naval Battle: An Eyewitness Account." Ships, 1962. 11 pp.

   This is a history of the seaplane tender HALF MOON in the period October-December 1944. The first part recounts "a view of a major naval engagement from the 50-yard line" at Surigao Straits in the Philippines in October 1944. The subsequent chronology describes support operations and air attacks. It is an interesting view of war from the perspective of a support ship.

186.   Hamilton, T. H. ENS, "The Navy and Physical Fitness in World War II." Individual Personnel, 1943. 17 pp. Appendices.

A mid-war report on the Navy's physical fitness program, concentrating on programs and organization. Appendices include a curriculum which was used at a physical instructor's school and the Physical Fitness Manual for the U.S. Navy.

187.   Harkness, Albert Jr., LTJG, "Retreat in the Southwest Pacific," part II of Pacific Area Command History Forces, n.d. 121 pp.

This study concentrates on the administrative organization, relations between commands, and strategic planning behind operations in the Southwestern Pacific during 1942-1943. The account is well organized and contains a table of contents. The preliminary draft of this study which is filed with this study contains a section entitled "Supplementary Data," which includes a calendar of important correspondence and a bibliography.

188.   Hart, Franklin A., COL, USMC, "Narrative Report of the Dieppe Raid, August 19, 1942." Individual Personnel, 27 August 1942. 7 pp. Appendices.

Colonel Hart was a U.S. Naval Attache in London when he submitted this account of the British commando raid on Dieppe.

189.   Hartford, Connecticut, Inspector of Naval
Material, "History of the Office of Inspector of
Naval Material, Hartford, Connecticut, World War
II." Shore Establishment, 1945. 22 pp. Appendices.

   This report briefly describes the functions
of the various departments within the Office of
the Inspector of Naval Material in Hartford. It
also provides more detailed examinations of major
problems encountered by the office during the war.
Appendices include lists of manufacturers producing
for the Navy in the Hartford, Bridgeport, and
Waterbury, Connecticut areas.

190.   Hayes, Grace P., LT, "The History of the Joint
Chiefs of Staff in World War II: The War Against
Japan." 2 vols., JCS, 1954. 952 pp. Appendices,
maps.

   Volume I, "Pearl Harbor Through Trident,"
describes the origins of decisions which directly
affected the war against Japan. Primary sources
for the study were JCS records. Vol. I. covers
the period from the Pearl Harbor attack to the
Trident Conference in May 1943. Volume II, "The
Advance to Victory," continues the study from May
1943 through Japan's surrender in August 1945.

191. Hayes, Thomas H., CDR (MC), "Bilibid Notebook." 2 vols., Individual Personnel, 12 July 1946. 154 pp. Illustrations, index.

This is a verbatim transcript of the personal journal kept by Commander Thomas H. Hayes, MC, USN, while he was Chief of Surgery in Bilibid Prison Hospital, Philippine Islands. It is a highly interesting account of a Navy doctor's experience as a Japanese prisoner of war.

192. Hayes, Thomas H., CDR (MC), "Hayes Report on Medical Tactics." Individual Personnel, 1946. 102 pp.

This is a collection of narrative histories of officers of the Medical, Dental, and Hospital Corps of the United States Navy on duty with the 4th Regiment, USMC in the Manila Bay area, especially following their capture by the Japanese.

193. Headlee, Colin D., CAPT, "U.S.S. DELTA (AR-9)." Ships, July 1952. 22 pp.

A history of Fleet Repair Ship DELTA, from her conversion in late 1942 to April 1944. Written with enthusiasm, this history relates how DELTA assisted in the Mediterranean landing campaigns.

194.	Hendricks, Daniel E., Jr., CAPT, "History of the U.S. Naval Reserves Participation in Cuban Revolt of 1933." Individual Personnel, n.d. 3 pp. Appendices.

　　This is a brief factual narrative of the expedition of CLAXTON, a reserve destroyer based in New Orleans, to Havana in response to civil disturbances in 1933. The author was an officer on board CLAXTON at the time. Appendices are newspaper accounts of the operation.

195.	Hern, Thomas F., LT, "History of Assistant Industrial Manager's Office, San Pedro, California." Shore Establishment, 1946. 3 pp. Charts.

　　A brief sketch of the post of Assistant Industrial Manager at San Pedro, California, from the establishment of the position in July 1940 through the end of 1945.

196.	Hern, Thomas F., LT, "History of U.S. Naval Drydocks, Terminal Island Naval Shipyard." Shore Establishment, 1946. 181 pp. Appendices, maps, charts.

　　A complete study of the Terminal Island facility and surrounding area dating back to Spanish usage of the area in the early 19th century and ending with the signing of the armistice with Japan.

197.	Hewitt, H. Kent, ADM, "The Navy in the European Theater of Operations in World War II." Individual Personnel, 1947. 53 pp. Maps.

This presentation, made at the Naval War College, in January 1947, discusses in some detail the amphibious invasions by the allied navies during such operations as Torch, Overlord, Husky, Avalanche, and Dragoon.

198.	Historical Section, Office of the Chief of Naval Operations, "United States Naval Administration in World War II, History of the Naval Armed Guard." CNO, 1946. 253 pp.

The manuscript covers all theaters of the war from the North Russian Run to the Indian Ocean. The names of individuals have, generally speaking, been omitted. The study utilized the complete files of the Armed Guard Service.

199.	Hoffman, Roy C., LCDR, "Report on Lend-Lease Activities in the Department of the Navy Before and During World War II." Admin. Hist. Appen. Procurement and Material 22, 27 July 1948. 16 pp. Appendices.

A brief summary. See also entry 421.

200.	Holland, W. D., "History of the Port Director's Office Eniwetok." Admin. Hist. Appen. 18 (D), 7 November 1945. 17 pp. Appendices.

    This is a contemporary description of the island and its military organization and a brief narrative of activities from about May 1944.

201.	Hollingshead, Billie, 2nd LT. USMCWR, "The Japanese Attack of 7 December 1941 on the Marine Corps Air Station at Ewa, Oahu, Territory of Hawaii." USMC, January 1945. 34 pp. Maps.

    A description of the raid and its aftermath in relation to the Marine Corps Air Station.

202.	Hollywood, Florida, Naval Training School (Tactical Radar), "History of CIC Training at USNTS (Tactical Radar), Hollywood, Florida." Admin. Hist. Appen. 30 (2), 30 October 1945. 19 pp.

    This account traces the development of instruction in the tactical employment of radar from March 1944 through the war's end.

203.   Horne, Charles F., CAPT, "Report of a Board Convened by the Commander in Chief, U.S. Pacific Fleet, to Make Recommendations on Radio Equipment Based on Experience in the War Which Resulted in the Defeat of Japan." Individual Personnel, 1 November 1945. 146 pp.

This report of the lessons concerning the use of radio during World War II gives recommendations for future development.

204.   Horne, Charles F., CAPT, "Report of Board Convened to Consider and Report on Radar and Countermeasures Equipment." Individual Personnel, 6 November 1945. 142 pp.

This board was set up after World War II to consider the lessons learned in the use of radar in combat. It makes various recommendations for the development of Naval and Marine Corps radar.

205.   Horne, Frederick J., VADM, "Report of the Board to Study Matters Concerning Regular and Reserve Personnel of the Navy and Marine Corps." Individual Personnel, November 1940. 57 pp.

This is an analysis of the needs and requirements of the Navy regarding personnel during the military buildup preceding Pearl Harbor. In this report, detailed assumptions of manpower requirements for the entire naval establishment are presented.

206.	Hunters Point, California, Naval Training Center, "Command History." Admin. Hist. Appen. 21 (14), n.d. 32 pp. Appendices.

This is a study of wartime training conducted in World War II while ships were involved in shipyard maintenance.

207.	Hurt, Samuel H., CAPT, "Battle For Leyte Gulf." Individual Personnel, 1945. 39 pp.

A lecture at the Naval War College on 23 May 1945 which presents a detailed narrative of the battle.

I

208.	Iceland Naval Operating Base, "Administrative History of the Naval Operating Base, Iceland." Shore Establishment, 23 October 1945. 41 pp. Illustrations.

This account presents a general examination of the command structure of U.S. Naval Forces in Iceland and the North Atlantic, the political and military factors behind the establishment of American bases in Iceland, and the construction of the American Naval facilities there. Although the operations of the N.O.B. are not covered, the history provides a good explanation of the importance of the base.

209.   INDIANA (BB-58), Aviation Unit, "History of Aviation Unit, U.S.S. INDIANA (BB-58)." Ships, 1945. 14 pp. Appendices.

This short unit history covers the period 30 April 1942 to 31 December 1944, with a supplement covering 1 January - 30 March 1945. The ship was active in the Pacific Theater.

210.   Intelligence Division, Office of the Chief of Naval Operations, "Combat Narrative." CNO-ONI, 1942-1945. 2290 pp.

Combat narratives were written to fill a temporary requirement before the appearance of official and semiofficial histories. The material originally appeared in classified publications or in nonpublished form as noted below:

Published:

"The Aleutians Campaign, June 1942 - August 1943," 105 pp.

"The Battle of the Coral Sea 4-8 May 1942," 60 pp.

"The Java Sea Campaign, " 92 pp.

"The Assault on Kwajalein and Majuro," (Part I), 92 pp.

"The Battle of Midway, 3-6 June 1942," 60 pp.

"The Landings in North Africa, November, 1942," 85 pp.

"Early Raids in the Pacific Ocean, 1 February - 10 March 1942," 71 pp. (Marshall and Gilbert Islands, Rabaul, Wake and Marcus, Lae and Salamaua.)

"Solomon Islands Campaign," 1200 pp.

    I. "The Landing in the Solomons, 7-8 August 1942."

    II. "The Battle of Savo Island, 9 August 1942."

    III. "The Battle of the Eastern Solomons, 23-25 August 1942."

    IV. "The Battle of Cape Esperance, 11 October 1942."

    V. "Battle of Santa Cruz Islands, 26 October 1942."

    VI. "Battle of Guadalcanal, 11-15 November 1942."

    VII. "Battle of Tassafaronga, 30 November 1942."

    VIII. "Japanese Evacuation of Guadalcanal, 29 January-8 February 1943."

    IX. "Bombardments of Munda and Vila - Stanmore, January-May 1943."

    X. "Operations in the New Georgia Area, 21 June-5 August 1943."

    XI. "Kolombangara and Vella Lavella, 6 August-7 October 1943."

XII. "The Bougainville Landing and the Battle of Empress Augusta Bay, 27 October-2 November 1943."

XIII. "The Sicilian Campaign, 10 July-17 August 1943."

"Miscellaneous Actions in the South Pacific, 8 August 1942-22 January 1943," 70 pp.

Non-Published Accounts:

"Anti-Aircraft Action, April 7, 1943, Guadalcanal-Tulagi," 110 pp.

"The Capture of the Gilberts," n.d., 75 pp.

"Convoy to Gaeta," 1944, 11 pp.

"Guadalcanal and Tulagi Bases," n.d., 102 pp.

"Japanese Attacks on Shipping in the Guadalcanal-Tulagi Area, 1943," 85 pp.

"The Movement of Supplies into the Guadalcanal-Tulagi Area," n.d., 22 pp.

"Operations in the Marianas Phase I: The Conquest of Saipan," n.d., 65 pp.

"Operations in the New Guinea Waters," n.d., 147 pp.

"The Salerno Landings, September 1943," 75 pp. Appendices.

"The Mediterranean Convoys," n.d., 33 pp.

"Pearl Harbor," 1942, 37 pp.

"The Navy's Share in the Tokyo Raid," n.d., 8 pp.

"Solomon Islands Campaign: XIII Bougainville Operations," 1943, 120 pp.

211. Intelligence Division, Office of the Chief of Naval Operations, "The Japan Sea." CNO, May 1945. 51 pp. Maps, illustrations.

This is a World War II intelligence analysis of the subject, stressing geography, navigation, and Japanese order of battle in the area.

212. Intelligence Division, Office of the Chief of Naval Operations, "Study of Italian Navy Including German Navy Operating in Mediterranean." CNO, 1 May 1943. 57 pp.

This is an intelligence analysis of Axis forces in the Mediterranean during World War II.

213. Ipitanga, Brazil, Naval Air Facility, "History of Naval Air Facility, Ipitanga." Admin. Hist. Appen. 24 (32), n.d. 25 pp. Appendices, photographs.

This brief chronological summary of the facility from 4 November 1943 to mid-1945 is augmented by appendices consisting mainly of instructions and directives.

214.   Iwo Jima Naval Base, "Base History of the Naval Base on Iwo Jima." Admin. Hist. Appen. 38 (16) (B), 13 October 1945. 14 pp. Charts.

This is a narrative account of the mission, operational activities, and changing functions of the base through 1945.

J

215.   Jeffersonville, Indiana, Supervisor of Shipbuilding, "History of the Office of the Supervisor of Shipbuilding, USN, Jeffersonville, Indiana." Shore Establishment, 13 February 1946. 18 pp.

In addition to excellent quantification of production levels this history has a section concerning problems encountered due to flooding along the Ohio River.

216.   Joint Army-Navy Air Transport Committee, "Report of Sub-committee on Pacific Air Transport Programs." 2 vols., Joint Commands, 15 July 1945. 130 pp. Appendices, maps, charts, index.

   Volume One is basically three large appendices containing background information and pertinent directives relating to the coordination of Army and Navy air transport services in the Pacific area during World War II. Volume Two contains annexes A through TT consisting of related maps and documents.

217.   [Joint] Army and Navy Munitions Board, "Survey of Congested War Production Areas." Joint Commands, 15 January 1943. 76 pp. Maps.

   This examines the conditions and problems found in Norfolk, Virginia; San Diego and Vallejo (Mare Island) California; and Portland, Maine during early wartime conditions in 1942. It contains an excellent introduction by Robert Moses. It provides valuable information on home front conditions during World War II.

218.   Joint Landing Force Board, Marine Barracks, Camp Lejeune, North Carolina, "Study the Conduct of Training of Landing Forces for Joint Amphibious Operations During World War II, to Include That Conducted in the Several Theaters of Operations, with the Objective of Determining the Nature, Organization and Scale of Effort Required and the Identification of the Major Problems Encountered." Joint Commands, May 1953. 103 pp. Appendices.

   This is a comprehensive history and analysis of joint amphibious operations in World War II conducted by U.S. Forces.

219.   Joint Purchasing Board, South Pacific Area, "Historical Data, United States Joint Purchasing Board, 1 January 1945 - 15 August 1945." Admin. Hist. Appen. 32 (1), n.d. 45 pp. Appendices, charts.

   This history outlines the supply activities of the U.S. Joint Purchasing Board.

220.   Junghans, Earl A., CAPT, "Wake: 1568-1946." Individual Personnel, n.d. 20 pp.

   This is an overall history of Wake Island during the period indicated. The great bulk of the account concerns the struggle between the U.S. and Japan over the Island during World War II. It was apparently written shortly after the Japanese surrender.

K

221. Karig, Walter, CAPT, "U.S. Navy Report on Guam, 1899-1950: History of Guam Under Naval Administration." Individual Personnel, 1950. 41 pp.

   This is a comprehensive history of the Navy's administration of Guam, that provides factual coverage of public health, education, agriculture, law and justice, and government. Also included is a brief history of Spanish colonial administration in Guam before 1898.

222. Kelley, Marion R., CAPT, "Chapters I-V of the History of the Applied Physics Laboratory, Johns Hopkins University." Individual Personnel, 1965. 321 pp.

   This is a thorough account of the development of several naval weapons systems over the past twenty years. The account includes chapters on the VT fuse and the Terrier, Triton, and Bumblebee missile programs.

223. Kelley, Marion R., CAPT, "Development of U.S. Navy Bases in the Southwest Pacific Area." Fleets, 1943. 41 pp.

   This report is a historical record of early naval base development in the Southwest Pacific, including the use of tenders and other support ships.

224.   Kelly, R. J., LT, LT S. B. Mitchell, LT W. B. Ashby and 1st LT J. D. Williams, USMC, "Command History, Eniwetok Atoll." Admin. Hist. Appen. 38 (31), 10 September 1945. 320 pp. Charts, appendices, photographs.

   This thorough research effort traces the island's history from its occupation in early 1944 to the establishment of N.O.B. Eniwetok in June 1945.

225.   Kentner, Robert W., PhM1, "Kentner's Journal: Bilibid Prison, Manila, P.I. from December 8, 1941 to February 25, 1945." Individual Personnel, 1945. 155 pp. Illustrations.

   This is a daily journal of events connected with the personnel of the U.S. Naval Hospital Canacao, Philippines, from the outbreak of the war in the Philippine Islands until the liberation of Bilibid Prison. The journal is mainly a daily chronicle of medical and personnel changes. Very complete records are given of the numbers and causes of death of those committed to the prison hospital while under Japanese occupation.

226.   Kittredge, Tracy B., CAPT, "Historical Monograph: U.S. - British Naval Cooperation, 1940 - 1945." Individual Personnel, n.d. 1,022 pp. Appendices.

   Despite its title, Captain Kittredge only completed this study through the end of 1941. The thorough, fully documented text covers the entire scope of relations, according to these major topics:

    I.   Policy and Strategy Background of U.S. Action in World War II.

    II. U.S. - British Relations, 1939 - 1940.

    III. Problems of U.S. Naval Aid to Britain: 1940.

    IV. Preparation of American-British War Plans.

    V.   Strategic Concepts and Victory Requirements (July - November 1941).

There is no overall index to this extensive monograph, but each major topic is divided into chapters.

227. Knox, Carl W., "A Narrative of Base Activities, United States Naval Air Facility, Sao Luiz, Brazil." Admin. Hist. Appen. 24 (24), 27 April 1945. 42 pp. Appendices, photographs.

    The narrative includes both a chronology and narrative summary of operations from 15 April 1943 to 15 April 1945.

228. Koeler, John T., "General Memorandum Concerning Organization and Operation of Advanced Base Unit 2." Individual Personnel, 28 June 1943. 12 pp.

    This document outlines the preparations of Advanced Base Unit 2 for the invasion of Sicily in 1943.

229.   Kohl, Jessie W., "History of the Medical Research Department, U.S. Submarine Base, New London, Connecticut, 7 December 1941 to 7 December 1945." Shore Establishment, 7 December 1945. 64 pp.

Mrs. Kohl's history of the Medical Research Department in New London is primarily administrative, covering the origins, development, and functions of the department and its several schools; Submarine Escape Training School, Lookout Training School, School for Pharmacists Mates Entering the Submarine Service, School for Second Class Divers, and Interior Voice Communications School.

230.   Kraker, George P., CAPT, "Report of Board to Evaluate and Make Recommendations on Ordnance Matters as the Result of War Experiences." Individual Personnel, November 1945. 84 pp.

A report for the Commander-In-Chief, U.S. Pacific Fleet of lessons learned regarding naval ordnance during World War II and the changes that should be made in light of these lessons. This report includes information on weapons procurement.

231.   Kralovec, Dalibor W., LT, "A Naval History of Espiritu Santo, New Hebrides." 2 vols., Shore Establishment, 1945. 783 pp. Maps, illustrations.

Lieutenant Kralovec's history is a comprehensive account of a major advanced base in World War II. Scholarly as well as thorough, the study traces the history and geography of the New Hebrides, the effect of the war on the islands, and the establishment and operation of the Advanced Naval Base. Footnotes are extensive, although a bibliography is lacking. The text is amplified with photographs and supplementary tables.

232.   Kwajalein Naval Base, "Command History of U.S. Naval Base Kwajalein." Admin. Hist. Appen. 38 (16) (C), 13 October 1945. 220 pp. Charts, photographs.

This comprehensive document covers every phase of the Kwajalein base from its inception in late 1943 to July 1945.

L

233.   Land, William G., and Adrian O. Van Wyen, "Naval Air Operations in the Marianas." Individual Personnel, 1945. 165 pp.

This analysis of the Marianas Operation, culminating in the "Marianas Turkey Shoot" of 19-20 June 1944, presents a wealth of factual and statistical information relating to both the preparatory operations and the operations themselves. Drawn entirely from primary sources (chiefly official publications, dispatches, and reports), the study is supported by numerous statistical tables.

234.   LCS (L) (3) 61, "Ship's History of U.S.S. LCS (L) (3) 61." Ships, 20 August 1945. 10 pp.

This is a brief command history of a landing craft support vessel commissioned in November 1944, which saw much action at Okinawa. It contains a roster of the crew.

235.   LCS (L) (3) 92, "Ship's History of U.S.S. LCS (L) (3) 92." Ships, 28 September 1945. 3 pp.

The period covered in this brief history is January to October 1945. The ship participated in the Okinawa Campaign during this period.

236.   Leap, Clifford R., LT (CEC), "Historical Data of Naval Base, Milne Bay, New Guinea." Admin. Hist. Appen. 34 (35), 10 October 1945. 41 pp. Maps.

A well organized study covering initial development through postwar demobilization.

237.   Leopold, Richard W., LT, "Fleet Organization, 1919 - 1941." Individual Personnel, 1945. 42 pp.

A synopsis of the origin, designation, and disestablishment of major fleets, permanent task forces, and fleets in the United States Navy; permanent task forces outside the United States Fleet; and type commands. An excellent guide to naval fleet organization during this period.

238.	Levin, Sol, Y3c(T), "Historical Record of Group Pacific Twelve." Admin. Hist. Appen. 38 (16) (F), 15 October 1945. 20 pp. Chart.

　　This is a narrative account of Gropac Twelve from its commissioning on December 8, 1944 to its landing at Ie Shima in mid-1945. Gropac [Group Pacific] components were charged with establishing and maintaining harbors and ports at advanced bases, administering troop arrivals and directing ship traffic.

239.	Leyte-Samar, Philippines, Naval Operating Base, "History of Roll Up and Disestablishment." Shore Establishment, n.d. 44 pp. Illustrations.

　　This facility was one of the principal supply bases during the latter part of the war in the Western Pacific. The account relates the problems and achievements at this site revolving about the rapid demobilization of U.S. Forces at the end of the war.

240.	Logistic Organizational Planning Unit, Office of the Chief of Naval Operations, "Governmental Organization for Industrial Mobilization, World War II." CNO, n.d. 33 pp.

　　Covering the period 1939 to 1942, the narrative traces the difficulties of the government in meeting the industrial and economic crises of the war effort. The activities of the War Resources Administration and the Office of Emergency Management represent the focus of this study.

241.   London, Naval Dispensary, "U.S. Naval Dispensary, London." Shore Establishment, n.d. 4 pp.

    The rough draft of a brief history of the Naval dispensary in London, which provided outpatient care for the Navy, Army, and Embassy personnel in London.

242.   Loomis, Alfred F., CDR, "A Short History of Mine Sweeping, Fourth Naval District." Admin. Hist. Appen. 45 (1), February 1944. 28 pp.

    This readable, first-person account was written by the commanding officer of the Mine Sweeping Group in the Fourth Naval District during part of World War II (August 1942 - February 1944).

243.   Lord, Clifford L., LCDR, "The History of Naval Aviation, 1898 - 1939 (rough draft)." Individual Personnel, 1946. 1438 pp.

    This is a detailed, comprehensive, and thoroughly documented account of U.S. Naval Aviation. A shorter, undocumented version of this work by Archibald D. Turnbull and Lord was published by the Yale University Press in 1949.

244.   LSM Group Five, "The History of LSM Group Five Staff Aboard the U.S.S. LSM 36." Type Commands, 1945. 18 pp.

   This brief account of LSM Group Five describes landings in the Dutch East Indies, in addition to the major operations in Lingayen Gulf and at Mindanao in the Philippines. The period covered is June 1944 to December 1945. This account appears to capture the spirit of amphibious operations. It is undocumented but has useful sectional headings which make for easy reference.

245.   LST Flotilla 3, "Early History of LST Flotilla Three." Type Commands, n.d. 2 pp.

   This is a brief account of the operations of this unit in the Aleutians and in the Kiska campaigns.

246.   LST Flotilla 7, "History of LST Flotilla Seven." Type Commands, 1946. 21 pp.

   This is an account of this unit's operations at Australia, New Guinea, Kiriwina and Goodenough Islands, Cape Gloucester, Admiralty Islands, Hollandia, Leyte Gulf, Mindoro, Lingayen, and Corregidor.

247.   LST Flotilla 13, "War History of LST Flotilla Thirteen." Type Commands, 1945. 20 pp.

    This brief account of operations includes both a chronology, beginning in August 1943, and a staff roster. The Flotilla's operations were at Saipan, Eniwetok, Tinian, Guadalcanal, Peleliu, Iwo Jima, Philippines, Japan, and Guam.

248.   LST Flotilla 31, "History of LST Flotilla Thirty-One." Type Commands, 1946. 4 pp.

    This is a very brief account of this unit's operations, commencing 9 January 1945. Too late to see wartime action, the unit operated in the Hawaiian, Philippines, and Marianas areas.

249.   LST Flotilla 32, "History of LST Flotilla Thirty-Two." Type Commands, 1945. 12 pp.

    This is a brief account of this unit's operations, commencing 25 January 1945, in the area of the Hawaiian Islands, Eniwetok, Saipan, Leyte, Yokohama, and Guam.

250.   LST Flotilla 34, "War History: Commander LST Flotilla Thirty-Four." Type Commands, 1946. 7 pp.

    This is a brief account of this unit's operations commencing April 1945 and includes a chronology of visits to Guam, Hawaii, Eniwetok, the Philippines, and Japan.

251.   LST Flotilla 35, "History of LST Flotilla Thirty-Five." Type Commands, 1946. 5 pp.

This is a brief account of this unit's operations from December 1944 to April 1946 in the Pacific Theater.

252.   LST Flotilla 36, "History of The Command, LST Flotilla Thirty-Six." Type Commands, n.d. 12 pp.

This is a brief account of this unit's operations in which some ships were ordered to Okinawa while others went to Guam and Eniwetok. The Flotilla which made visits to Leyte and Subic Bay, saw little enemy action.

253.   LST Group 102, "War History of Commander, LST Group One Hundred-Two." Type Commands, 1946. 3 pp.

This is a brief account of the unit, which was commissioned 11 June 1945. The group did not see combat action in the Pacific Ocean campaigns.

254.   LST Group 108, "The History of the Command of LST Group One Hundred-Eight." Type Commands, n.d. 5 pp.

This is a very brief account of this unit's operations. Commissioned in March 1945, this group operated in the Pacific Ocean areas but did not participate in combat actions.

Mc

255.   McCleary, Eugene E., LTJG, "History of U.S. Naval Advanced Base, Guadalcanal, 1942-1945." 2 vols., Shore Establishment, 1945. Appendices, maps, index.

Volume I of the history is a solid, well-organized record of the organization and activities of the advanced base. All aspects are thoroughly discussed, including command relations, operations, logistics, and the physical characteristics of the island. The history has an index and appendices, although bibliographical documentation is generally lacking. Appendices present personnel and equipment statistics. Volume II contains command histories prepared by the following units attached to the Base: Boat Operating and Repair Unit; Construction Battalion Maintenance Units 518, 520, and 533; Fleet Hospital 108; and Naval Landing Force Equipment Depot.

256.   McGovern, John B., RADM, "Transport Squadron Sixteen." Individual Personnel, 1945. 28 pp.

This squadron's role in the Iwo Jima and Okinawa campaigns is related. Over half the study is a discussion of administrative and staff command relationships and responsibilities.

257.   McKelvey, Carlton A., LCDR, "Construction of the U.S. Naval Air Station, L'Aber Vrach, France, World War I." Individual Personnel, 1963. 25 pp.

This paper is an interesting account of the establishment of a World War I seaplane base. Lieutenant Commander McKelvey was commanding officer of the construction force.

258.   McPherson, Guy and Mary Walls, "Fixing Wages and Salaries of Navy Civilian Employees in Shore Establishments, 1862-1945." Administrative Reference Service Reports No. 9, Washington: Department of the Navy, May 1945. 13 pp.

The study briefly mentions the basic act regulating hours and wages that was approved 16 July 1862 and the subsequent changes to 1945.

259.   McWhorter, Thomas, LCDR, "Stand and Fight: The Story of A Destroyer In Battle." Ships, 1945. 126 pp.

This account of the wartime career of STERETT by one of her officers describes STERETT's operations during escort duty in the Atlantic, reinforcement of Malta, and the Guadalcanal Campaign until the ship was damaged during the Battle of Guadalcanal, 12 - 13 November 1942.

M

260. Madden, George B., RADM, "Loss of LITTLE and GREGORY." Individual Personnel, n.d. 4 pp.

This narrative describes the combat loss of two APD's in the Solomons area during August 1942. The author was commanding officer of one of the ships in company with those lost.

261. Madison, Wisconsin, Naval Training School, University of Wisconsin, "Administrative History of the Radio School at the University of Wisconsin at Madison." Admin. Hist. Appen. 30 (1), 21 July 1945. 18 pp. Appendix.

This narrative summary devotes attention to the problems encountered in operating a Navy radio school on a university campus during World War II.

262. Maracaibo, Venezuela, American Consulate, "Report Regarding Submarine Activities in the Gulf of Venezuela Area." Shore Establishment, 1942, 14 pp.

This contains several pieces of correspondence related to the initiation of German submarine shelling of ships in the Gulf plus oil refineries on the island of Aruba. It incorporates information on Venezuelan reaction to German activities.

263.   Mare Island Naval Shipyard, "History of Mare Island Navy Yard in World War II." Shore Establishment, 1946. 321 pp. Appendices, maps.

The narrative is divided into six parts: (I) Organization of the Yard, (II) Facilities, (III) Repair Work, (IV) New Production, (V) Labor and Management and (VI) Accounting and Other Controls. Part IV on New Production is particularly useful for its complete data, while part V discusses labor problems and policies at the 42,300-man establishment. The role and contribution of women to the war effort is described briefly. Letters, orders, messages, and other primary sources are located in the work.

264.   Marianas Command, "Permanent Communication and Electronic Facilities Guam." Naval Forces, October 1945. 59 pp. Illustrations.

This technical report discusses electronics and communications installations.

265.   Marine Corps Headquarters, Historical Division, "The Bougainville Operation." USMC, n.d. 44 pp. Appendices.

This account of the Bougainville operation, which spans the period from 1 November to 28 December 1943, was compiled from official records of the First Marine Amphibious Corps, the Third Marine Division, and regiments. Few reports of battalion level or lower units were used. The narrative is concerned with operations of the ground forces of the Third Marine Division and the 37th Division, U.S. Army, and of the First Marine Amphibious Corps in setting up the beachhead. The appendices include rosters of commanding officers and staff as well as a casualty report.

266.   Marine Corps Headquarters, Historical Division, "First Marine Division, 1941-1945." USMC, n.d. 34 pp.

   The narrative gives a brief outline of the problems in training, equipping, and quartering during the division's expansion from a small prewar nucleus to a brigade and finally to a war strength division. The history relates the four-month period of continuous fighting in the Guadalcanal-Tulagi area; rest and re-equipping in Australia; operations in New Britain and the Peleliu Island campaigns; and finally rehearsals, training, and the ultimate invasion of Okinawa.

267.   Marine Corps Headquarters, Intelligence Section, Division of Aviation, "Marine Air Intelligence Bulletin, August - September 1945." USMC, 1945. 28 pp. Maps, illustrations.

   This bulletin contains a historical summary of Marine Corps air actions on Okinawa and throughout World War II.

268.   Marine Corps Headquarters, Intelligence Section, Division of Aviation, "Marine Dive Bombers in the Philippines." USMC, 5 May 1945. 15 pp.

   This is a brief analysis and summary of the operations of USMC squadrons based on Luzon, Philippines for the month of February 1945. Data were obtained from war diaries and air combat action reports of the squadrons.

269.	Marine Corps Headquarters, Intelligence Section, Division of Aviation, "Marine Fighter Squadrons in the Philippines." USMC, June 1945. 15 pp.

　　This is a summary and analysis of the activities of two Marine fighter groups from February through April 1945.

270.	Marshalls - Gilberts Area, Military Government Section, "A Report On the U.S. Navy Military Government of the Marshall Islands For the Year 31 January 1944 to 31 January 1945." Naval Forces, 1945. 38 pp. Maps, appendices.

　　This report is a history of U.S. Naval administration for the period indicated. The Marshalls were the first Japanese mandated islands to be occupied and placed under U.S. military administration during the war.

271.	Marshalls - Gilberts Patrol and Escort Group, "Wartime History of Task Group 96.3." Admin. Hist. Appen. 18 (E), 28 August 1945. 7 pp. Appendices.

　　This is a brief history of the major events and command relationships of Task Group 96.3 which provided convoy protection between the Marshall Islands and forward area ports, provided patrol craft for Marshalls-Gilberts bases, and conducted anti-submarine warfare.

272.   MASSACHUSETTS (BB-59), Aviation Unit, "History of Aviation Unit, U.S.S. MASSACHUSETTS (BB-59)." Ships, 1945. 95 pp. Appendices, illustrations.

This is a full history of a World War II Battleship Aviation Unit during the period May 1942-July 1945. The report provides a comprehensive account of operations, personnel, and the concept of such units.

273.   Medicine and Surgery Bureau, Hospital Corps Archives, "Hospital Corps Archives, HC Archives Final Memo 218-46." Shore Establishment, 27 September 1946. 25 pp.

This report provides a brief summary of the accomplishments of the Hospital Corps Archives Unit. More important is the inventory of the numerous documents, many relating to conditions in prisoner of war camps, and other memorabilia which were collected by the unit over five years. Disposition of the material is indicated.

274.   Medicine and Surgery Bureau, Hospital Corps Archives, "Rules and Regulations for Prisoners of War." Shore Establishment, 25 March 1946. 21 pp.

This is a collection of twelve documents salvaged from various Japanese prisoner-of-war camps by Pharmacist Mate First Class Robert Kentner. Documents contain rules, regulations, and statements of policy promulgated by both Japanese and American authorities at the Cabanatuan, Pasay School concentration camp and Bilibid Camps from 1942 to 1944.

275. Mickler, Joseph R., LCDR, "Key West in World War II; A History of the Naval Station and Naval Operating Base." Shore Establishment, September 1945. 176 pp. Appendices.

Lieutenant Commander Mickler's command history of Naval Station, Key West is essentially an administrative history, dwelling extensively on the organization of the station and its construction after reopening in 1939. Relations with the civilian community in Key West are discussed. The history also provides a review of mine and submarine warfare in the Key West and Gulf areas. A brief history of Key West and the Naval Station from its establishment in 1822 is included.

276. Miller, R. D., Flight Lieutenant, Royal New Zealand Air Force, "Narrative of Personal Experiences of War Experiences in the Far East." Individual Personnel, n.d. 70 pp. Appendices.

A detailed description of prisoner of war life under the Japanese at various camps in the Far East, including Bandoeng, Batavia, Singapore, and Palembang where an air facility was built with British and Dutch labor.

277. Mine Warfare Section, Office of the Chief of Naval Operations, [History of U.S. Navy Mine and Bomb Disposal in World War II.] CNO, n.d. 53 pp.

The title page is missing and hence the subject is supplied from the introductory remarks. This history deals with mine and bomb disposal as coordinated and directed from the Mine Warfare Section. The history follows a general chronological order covering the period 1941-1945. The file of references used for footnoting is not attached.

278.   Mine Warfare Section, Office of the Chief of Naval Operations, "Offensive Mining Operations." CNO, 1941. 84 pp.

   This is a collection of documents containing contingency plans and assumptions for offensive mining operations in the Atlantic, Pacific, and Asiatic Theaters.

279.   MINNEAPOLIS (CA-36), Aviation Unit, "History of Aviation Unit, VCS-6, U.S.S. MINNEAPOLIS (CA-36)." Ships, 1945. 4 pp.

   This brief unit history covers the periods 1 January 1944 - 1 April 1945, and 5 July 1945- August 1945, during which time the ship took part in actions at Maloelap Atoll, Truk Island, Leyte, and Okinawa.

280.   MISSOURI (BB-63), Aviation Unit, "History of Aviation Unit, U.S.S. MISSOURI (BB-63)." Ships, 1945. 17 pp.

   This unit history contains two almost identical short narrative accounts of operations at Okinawa.

281.   Mobile Explosives Investigation Unit 4, "History of Mobile Explosives Investigation Unit 4." Shore Establishment, 5 September 1945. 7 pp. Appendices.

This short command history contains records of unit investigations and assaults on Tarawa, Guam, Saipan, Samar, Luzon, Iwo Jima, and Okinawa. Award commendations are included.

282.   Moore, George F., MGEN, USA, "Report on Philippine Coast Artillery Command and the Harbor Defenses of Manila and Subic Bays, Corregidor, 14 February 1941-6 May 1942." Individual Personnel, 1946. 148 pp. Appendices.

The report by General Moore, Commander of the Harbor Defenses around Corregidor, from 14 February 1941 until its surrender to Japan on 6 May 1942, provides a detailed appraisal of the preparation of the command for war and its performance in battle. Extensive appendices of reports, plans, and statistics are included. Several exhibits, notably maps and charts, have been omitted from this copy because of size. The chronological battle narrative was drawn chiefly from the Journal of the Harbor Defense Command Post Duty Officers and expanded by extracts from personal diaries and from records made by officers in prison camps.

283.   Moore, William C., LCDR, "History of Commander Service Force, United States Pacific Fleet." Type Commands, 1945. 361 pp.

This history deals mostly with the administrative and non-combat activities of the Service Force, Pacific, throughout the war. The author has used a topical approach, thereby allowing a rapid survey of any given area of interest such as Fleet Post Office, Medical Force, and Shore Patrol. A table of contents is included. The study is footnoted.

284.   Morro Bay, California, Amphibious Training Base, "History of Amphibious Training Base, Morro Bay, California." Admin. Hist. Appen. 3 (II), n.d. 25 pp.

This narrative account and description of the evolution of the base from its establishment on 16 November 1941 includes succinct accounts of the functions of each training group. This history is identified as an appendix to the "Command History of the Amphibious Forces Training Command."

285.   Motor Torpedo Boat Squadron 13, "History of the Motor Torpedo Boat Squadron Thirteen." Type Commands, 1945. 19 pp.

This brief account is the official history of the squadron. It discusses initial training and operational campaigns in the Aleutian and South Pacific Theaters.

286.   Motor Torpedo Boat Squadron 15, "Arabian Nights in the Mediterranean, A P.T. Odyssey," Type Commands, 1943. 67 pp.

　　　　This is a lighthearted history of Motor Torpedo Boat Squadron 15 for the year 1943. Organization, training, deployment, and matters of human interest are covered.

287.   Motor Torpedo Boat Squadron 31, "Command History-Motor Torpedo Boat Squadron Thirty-One." Type Commands, 1945. 2 pp.

　　　　This is a very brief description of the activities of the unit from 18 June 1945 to 11 July 1945 in the Okinawa Area.

288.   Motor Torpedo Boat Squadron 32, "History of MTB Squadron Thirty-Two." Type Commands, 6 November 1945. 15 pp. Tables.

　　　　Covering the period from 10 June 1944 to 18 December 1945, this history describes, in a chronological narrative, the operations of this unit in the Caribbean and the Western Pacific. Ammunition expenditures are listed.

289.   Motor Torpedo Boat Squadron 38, "History of MTB Squadron Thirty-Eight." Type Commands, 24 October 1945. 4 pp.

　　　　This account, which covers the period from 20 December 1944 to 24 October 1945, includes the activation, training, deployment to the Pacific, and combat operations of the unit.

290.   Motor Torpedo Boat Squadrons, Philippine Sea Frontier, "Command History of Motor Torpedo Boat Squadrons, Philippine Sea Frontier, Formerly Motor Torpedo Boat Squadrons, Seventh Fleet." 5 vols., Type Commands, 1945. 880 pp. Appendices.

This work discusses organization of the Motor Torpedo Boat Squadrons, as well as their operations in Eastern New Guinea, the Bismark Archipelago, Western New Guinea, and the Philippine areas. Concluding with an analysis, the work is complete and well organized. An excellent table of contents permits easy searching for specific information.

291.   MOUNT MC KINLEY (AGC-7), "History of U.S.S. MOUNT MC KINLEY (AGC-7)." Ships, n.d. 6 pp.

This short command history gives a summary of operations in the Pacific during 1944-1945.

292.   Mowry, George E., "Landing Craft and the War Production Board: April 1942 to May 1944." Admin. Hist. Appen. War Admin., 8 March 1946. 76 pp. Appendices.

In addition to recording the Board's involvement in landing craft production, this study analyzes the associated problems of overall industrial mobilization. Topics include implementation of armed service requirements into production requirements, the Board's relationship to procurement agencies, and the problem of making design changes after production had begun.

293.	Myers, Richard T., "The Saigon Raid." Individual Personnel, 1947. 4 pp.

   This is a recollection of the 12 January 1945 air raid by U.S. Navy planes against Saigon in Japanese- held Indo-China, written by a British artillery Sergeant, who was then a prisoner of war in Saigon.

<u>N</u>

294.	NASHVILLE (CL-43), Aviation Unit, "History of Aviation Unit, U.S.S. NASHVILLE (CL-43)." Ships, 25 November 1945. 2 pp.

   This is an extremely brief unit history, which includes information on operations at Wake Island, Biak, and Brunei Bay.

295.	Natal, Brazil, Naval Operating Facility, "Administrative History of Naval Operating Facility Natal, Brazil." Admin. Hist. Appen. 24 (21), n.d. 45 pp. Appendices.

   This is a carefully prepared and detailed summary of activities at this South Atlantic support facility from 14 October 1941 to mid-1945.

100

296.   National War College, "Joint Overseas Operations." 2 vols., Type Commands, 1946. 600 pp. (Approx.) Appendices.

This is the first part of a very extensive study of joint operational procedures and doctrines employed during World War II.

297.   Naval School of Military Government, Princeton University, "Report on the Naval School of Military Government." 7 vols., Type Commands, March 1945. 1559 pp. Appendices, maps.

A complete guide to this extensive and comprehensive survey of the Naval School at Princeton University is located in the table of contents. The report is a thorough description and analysis of the training of naval officers for civil and military government duties.

298.   Naval War College, Battle Analysis Series, Training Commands.

Each study in this series is a detailed tactical analysis based on information from both Allied and Japanese sources. The following items are included:

"The Battle for Leyte Gulf, October 1944." vols. I, II, III, and V, 1953-1958. 2,643 pp. Charts.

This study was not completed and covers only the period from 17 October to 25 October 1944.

"The Battle of the Coral Sea, May 1-11, 1942." 1947. 128 pp.

"The Battle of Midway, including the Aleutian Phase, June 3-14, 1942." 1948. 259 pp.

"The Battle of Savo Island, August 9, 1942." 1950. 378 pp. Charts.

299.   Naval War College, "The Battle of the Komandorski Islands." Type Commands, November 1943. 19 pp.

This is a detailed account of the 26 March 1943 daylight engagement in the Bering Sea between U.S. and Japanese surface forces.

300.   Navy School of Oriental Languages, University of Colorado, "The Navy School of Oriental Languages, University of Colorado, Boulder, Colorado." Type Commands, 1945. 36 pp.

This narrative treats the development of the Navy School of Oriental Languages, that began in 1941 at both Harvard and the University of California, Berkeley. The Harvard operation was terminated and the Berkeley group was transferred to Boulder because of relocation orders issued by the Western Defense Command to all persons of Japanese ancestry. The account stresses teaching techniques and methods employed.

301.   NEW ORLEANS (CA-32), Aviation Unit, "History of Aviation Unit, U.S.S. NEW ORLEANS (CA-32)." Ships, 1945. 25 pp. Appendices, illustrations.

Organized into a chronology, narrative, and appendix, this unit history covers the period 7 December 1941 - 31 December 1944 in the Pacific theater of operations.

302.   New York, New York, Inspector of Naval Material, "Historical Narrative, Office of the Inspector of Naval Material, New York." Admin. Hist. Appen. Procurement and Material 7, n.d. 173 pp. Appendices.

This history, which is a long, undocumented study of the functions of each section in the command's organization, shows how the war effort affected inspection procedures and policies.

303.   Newport, Rhode Island, Naval Hospital, "Historical Supplement to Fourth Quarterly Sanitary Report: Cumulative Report for Period of World War II, 7 December 1941 to 31 August 1945." Admin. Hist. Appen. 15 (YY), n.d. [September 1945]. 52 pp. Map, charts.

This detailed history traces the organization and experiences of a wartime hospital.

304.   Norfolk, Virginia, Assistant to The Industrial Manager, "History: Norfolk Navy Yard, September 1939 - September 1945." Shore Establishment, 1945. 406 pp. Maps, illustrations, index.

   In addition to a brief chronological narrative, this account contains numerous charts, graphs, messages, and letters. The primary emphasis is on a description of physical-plant capabilities and technical aspects of the shipyard, such as electronics and degaussing.

305.   Norfolk, Virginia, Naval Supply Depot, "War History, Naval Supply Depot Norfolk." Shore Establishment, 1945. 185 pp. Illustrations.

   Extensively illustrated, this war history is primarily an undocumented administrative history of the depot's activities during the war.

306.   Norfolk, Virginia, Naval Training School (Chaplains), "The Naval Training School (Chaplains), A Factual History." Admin. Hist. Appen. 42 (1), 15 November 1945. 14 pp. (p. 4 missing).

   A brief, well written account of the origin and development of the Chaplain's School during World War II. This history is identified as an appendix to the "History of the Office of the Director of Distribution, Fifth Naval District, N.O.B., Norfolk, Va."

307.	NORTH CAROLINA (BB-55), Aviation Unit, "History of Aviation Unit, U.S.S. NORTH CAROLINA (BB-55)." Ships, 1945. 3 pp.

This short unit history covers the period from May 1941 to May 1944.

308.	North Pacific Advanced Intelligence Center, "Aleutian Campaign: A Brief Historical Outline To and Including The Occupation of Kiska, August 1943." Naval Forces, 1944. 159 pp. Annexes.

This account covers the highlights of military preparations and operations in the North Pacific Area up to and including the climax of the Kiska operation in August 1943. Numerous photographs, maps, and charts add to the narrative. The numerous annexes are also useful, particularly in understanding planning. An interesting, but brief postscript includes information from a Japanese naval officer's diary on how the Japanese viewed the operation.

309.	North Pacific Naval Forces, "Command History, North Pacific Force." Naval Forces, 1945. 170 pp. Illustrations.

An introduction to this account contains an excellent geographical presentation which includes the overall picture of war in Alaska. American operations and planning throughout are well documented. Interesting illustrations and administrative flow charts are included.

310.	Norway, U. S. Naval Mission, "Historical Narrative of the U.S. Naval Component S.H.A.E.F. Mission to Norway." Naval Forces, 1946. 27 pp.

This brief but well organized history has a table of contents, an introduction, and a conclusion. The period covered by the account is late 1944-1945. The U.S. Naval Mission to Norway was small with only two officers assigned. Captain A.O.R. Bergesen headed the mission and also served as U.S. Naval Attache to Norway.

O

311.	Oahu, Hawaii, Combat Information Center School, "History of CIC School, Fleet Training Center, Oahu." Admin. Hist. Appen. 38 (14) (A), 15 September 1945. 700 pp. (approx). Appendices, photographs.

A twenty-five page annotated summary traces the school's development from the war's outbreak to its termination. Appendices include course curricula.

312.   Oahu, Hawaii, Fleet Training Center, "Fleet Training Center, Oahu, History; Annex A, Introduction." Shore Establishment, October 1945. 148 pp. Appendices, maps, illustrations, index.

This account traces the development of the Fleet Training Center, Oahu, by describing the evolution and eventual consolidation of various subordinate activities. Appendices are useful for tracing the early curriculum evolution at the Fleet Training Center.

313.   Oceanside, California, Amphibious Training Base, "History of Amphibious Training Base, Oceanside, California." Admin. Hist. Appen. 3 (III), n.d. 5 pp.

This history, which is identified as an appendix to the "Command History of the Amphibious Forces Training Command," briefly describes the major events of this base from late 1942 through 15 September 1945.

314.   Oceanside, California, Amphibious Training Base, "History of the Communications School, ATB, Oceanside, California." Admin. Hist. Appen. 3 (IV), n.d. 341 pp. Appendices, illustrations.

This detailed historical accounting of units trained at the school precedes a carefully written chronological narrative of the development and operation of the school. The appendices include course curricula.

315.	Office of Public Information, Department of Defense, "The Entry of the Soviet Union into the War Against Japan: Military Plans, 1941 - 1945." Cabinet, 1955. 107 pp.

This well-documented account of U.S.-Soviet relations in the Pacific during World War II makes excellent use of both primary and secondary sources.

316.	Okinawa Naval Operating Base, "Base History of N.O.B. Okinawa." Admin. Hist. Appen. 38 (29), 1945. 102 pp.

This base history has been divided into sections corresponding with the command's organization. A brief overview is contained in the initial three pages.

317.	Orange, Texas, Supervisor of Shipbuilding, "History of the Office of the Supervisor of Shipbuilding, USN, Orange, Texas." Shore Establishment, 1945. 21 pp. Appendices.

This work describes personnel assigned and specific tonnage and numbers of ships delivered by individual private shipyards in the Orange area.

P

318.   Pacific Beach, Hoquiam, Washington, Anti-Aircraft Training Center, "Command History: Anti-Aircraft Training Center, Pacific Beach, Hoquiam, Washington." Admin. Hist. Appen. 21 (11), n.d. 300 pp. Appendices.

   A brief narrative commencing 2 October 1942. Voluminous appendices contain course curricula.

319.   Pacific Fleet, "Annual Report of the Commander-in-Chief, U.S. Pacific Fleet, FY 1941." Fleets, 1941. 40 pp.

   Organization, operations and training, material, personnel, and inspections are discussed.

320.   Pacific Fleet, "Report of Operations in the Pacific Ocean Areas." Fleets, February 1942-December 1945. 3,000 pp. (approx). Charts, appendices.

   This month-by-month, detailed narrative of the War in the Pacific by the Fleet Commander, covers all major battles. Numerous tables, charts, and diagrams are included.

321.   Pacific Fleet and Pacific Ocean Area, Administrative Division, "History of the Administrative Division." Admin. Hist. Appen. CinCPac/Poa Analytical Div. 11, 5 October 1945. 250 pp. (approx). Appendices, charts, photographs.

   This extensive history is divided into eight sections along the lines of division organization. Only a brief general summary of the administrative division as a whole precedes the subordinate histories. Section narratives vary from historical accounts to outlines of administrative functions.

322.   Pacific Fleet and Pacific Ocean Area, Analytical Division, "Unity of Command as it Functioned in the Pacific Ocean Areas in World War II." Admin. Hist. Appen. CinCPac/Poa Analytical Div. 9, n.d. 35 pp.

   The narrative traces the genesis and development of CINCPOA as a joint command.

323.   Pacific Fleet and Pacific Ocean Area, "Command History, World War II, 7 December 1941 - 15 August 1945." Fleets, 1946. 445 pp.

   Written in topical form, the history discusses major tasks and responsibilities of CINCPAC-CINCPOA and describes the major command relationships as well as the channels by which the plans and orders reached operating forces. A general account of the character of the staff is followed by a description of the planning, operations, logistics, intelligence, communications, and internal administration sections. The volume is well documented. The appendices contain basic documents, such as staff instructions and directories, orders, letters, and memoranda.

324.   Pacific Fleet and Pacific Ocean Area, Communications Division, "History of CinCPac/CinCPoa Communications Division, 7 December 1941 - 15 August 1945." Admin. Hist. Appen. CinCPac/Poa Analytical Div. 13-14, 23 September 1945. 500 pp. (approx). Appendices, charts.

   In addition to histories of individual sections within the division, this comprehensive work contains an extensive general narrative of the division's role in the joint CINCPOA command.

325.   Pacific Fleet and Pacific Ocean Area, Intelligence Section, "A History of the Combat Intelligence Section, Staff CinC Pacific Fleet from December 7, 1941 until September 1945." Admin. Hist. Appen. CinCPac/Poa Analytical Div. 15-17, n.d. 450 pp. (approx). Appendices, charts, photographs.

   The narrative history of the Intelligence Section, as well as the Pacific Fleet Radio Unit (FRUPAC), covers six pages of this document. The balance contains extensive, detailed reports on psychological warfare activities in the Pacific Ocean area.

326.   Pacific Fleet and Pacific Ocean Area, Logistics Division, "Historical Data on Information, Fuel and Lubricants Section, Logistics Division, Joint Staff, CinCPoa." Admin. Hist. Appen. CinCPac/Poa Analytical Div. 22, n.d. 34 pp. Appendices, charts.

   The narrative section of this history covers the mission of the section as well as personnel assigned, policy matters, and concluding comments. The appendices include petroleum-use forecast indicators and charts of actual amounts dispensed.

327.   Pacific Fleet and Pacific Ocean Area, Logistics Division, "History of the Administrative and Statistical Section, Logistics Division." Admin. Hist. Appen. CinCPac/Poa Analytical Div. 18, 21 September 1945. 100 pp. (approx). Appendices, charts.

The narrative overview of the Administrative and Statistical Section covers ten pages of this document. Extensive appendices include reports, abstracted data, and equipment inventories.

328.   Pacific Fleet and Pacific Ocean Area, Logistics Division, "History of the Construction Section of the Logistics Division." Admin. Hist. Appen. CinCPac/Poa Analytical Div. 20, n.d. 150 pp. (approx). Appendices, charts.

This narrative summary deals with the mission, organization, and policies of the section and briefly explains the eighteen appendices that comprise the balance of the document.

329.   Pacific Fleet and Pacific Ocean Area, Logistics Division, "History of the Logistics Planning Section." Admin. Hist. Appen. CincPac/Poa Analytical Div. 25, n.d. 44 pp. Appendices, charts.

Divided into four parts covering organization, policy, section chronology, and concluding commentary, this report covers the period from January to August 1945.

330.   Pacific Fleet and Pacific Ocean Area, Logistics Division, "History of the Medical Section, Logistics Division, Joint Staff, CINCPAC/POA." Admin. Hist. Appen. CinCPac/Poa Analytical Div. 26, n.d. 53 pp. Appendices, charts.

   In addition to organizational and policy-oriented discussion, this history includes narrative summaries of the Preventive Medicine, Dental, and Military Government departments of the division.

331.   Pacific Fleet and Pacific Ocean Area, Logistics Division, "History of the Supply Section, Logistics Division, Staff CinCPoa." Admin. Hist. Appen. CinCPac/Poa Analytical Div. 24, n.d. 38 pp. Appendices, charts.

   This general account concentrates on mission and policy.

332.   Pacific Fleet and Pacific Ocean Area, Logistics Division, "History of the Transportation Section, Logistics Division." Admin. Hist. Appen. CinCPac/Poa Analytical Div. 23, 16 October 1945. 60 pp. Appendices, charts.

   This comprehensive study covers the entire scope of the section's operations in an especially well written and organized presentation.

333.   Pacific Fleet and Pacific Ocean Area, Military Government Section, "CINCPAC--CINCPOA Command History, Military Government Section." Admin. Hist. Appen. CinCPac/Poa Analytical Div. 29-30, n.d. 225 pp. (approx).

   In addition to a comprehensive overview of this section's role in CINCPAC/POA, this thorough history includes chronological summaries for operations in the Marshalls, Marianas, Western Carolines, and other campaigns. Detailed analyses of these projects and their effectiveness are included in the narrative.

334.   Pacific Fleet and Pacific Ocean Area, Operations Division, "History of the Operations Division." Admin. Hist. Appen. CinCPac/Poa Analytical Div. 31, 8 October 1945. 225 pp. (approx). Appendices, charts, photographs.

   Rather than a comprehensive history dealing with the role of the Operations Division, this document assembles summaries of the eight sections which comprised the division.

335.   Pacific Fleet and Pacific Ocean Area, Public Information Office, "History of CINCPAC Public Information." Admin. Hist. Appen. CinCPac/Poa Analytical Div. 42-43, n.d. 60 pp. Appendices.

   Carefully written and organized, this history places the establishment of CINCPAC's office in 1941 within the context of the Navy's overall public information program. The study includes coverage of the difficulties in disseminating news and information to the U.S. under wartime restraints and presents a thorough discussion of relationships with U.S. press representatives during the Pacific War.

336.   Pacific Fleet and Pacific Ocean Area, War Plans Division, "History of the War Plans Division During World War II." Admin. Hist. Appen. CinCPac/Poa Analytical Div. 40, 11 October 1945. 13 pp. Appendices.

The development of the section is traced from 7 December 1941 to 14 August 1945, during which it evolved from a Pacific Fleet planning agency to an joint organization with representatives from all services in the Pacific.

337.   Pacific Fleet and Pacific Ocean Area, Welfare and Recreation Section, "History of the Welfare and Recreation Section." Admin. Hist. Appen. CinCPac/Poa Analytical Div. 39, n.d. 9 pp. Appendices.

Deals exclusively with recommendations made by the section to the staff of CINCPAC/POA during the period 7 May - 10 October 1945.

338.   Pearl Harbor, Hawaii, Navy Yard, "History of Pearl Harbor Navy Yard." 4 vols., Shore Establishment, 1945. 1195 pp. Illustrations.

The narrative text of this history is largely limited to a brief summary of the history of the Navy Base at Pearl Harbor prior to the attack in 1941. The text is built around the hundreds of documents contained in the history. These include reports, letters, speeches, maps, blueprints, and photographs covering the attack, the subsequent restoration of ships and facilities, and the wartime operation and administration of the Navy Yard.

339.   Peleliu Naval Base, "Base History of U. S. Naval Base, Peleliu." Admin. Hist. Appen. 38 (16) (H), 8 October 1945. 5 pp.

   A brief narrative of the activities of the base from its commissioning on 22 March 1944.

340.   PENSACOLA (CA-24), Aviation Unit, "History of Aviation Unit, U.S.S. PENSACOLA (CA-24)." Ships, 1945. 8 pp. Appendices.

   This is a short narrative summary of operations in the Pacific Theater throughout the war.

341.   [Personnel, Bureau of Naval], "Annual Report of the Chief of the Bureau of Navigation for the Fiscal Year 1941." Shore Establishment, 4 September 1941. 88 pp. Appendices.

   Admiral Nimitz's report is a valuable record of the rapid buildup of the Navy's manpower during the months prior to Pearl Harbor. Beginning with a chronological synopsis of the legislative and administrative steps taken to implement this buildup, the report provides coverage of the problems associated with the task of converting a relatively small peacetime organization into a large, mobilized force ready for war. Much space is devoted to the mobilization and training of the revitalized Naval Reserve. Extensive statistical evidence is provided.

342.   Personnel, Bureau of Naval Officer Training Section, "History of Navy Chemical Warfare Training After World War I." Admin. Hist. Appen. 30 (2), 9 August 1944. 11 pp.

   A major problem was the shortage of students due to the extended operating schedules of fleet units and a reluctance to send senior officers for training.

343.   Personnel, Bureau of Naval, "Training Aids in World War II." Shore Establishment, n.d. 27 pp. Appendices.

   The report centers on the Navy's lack of training aids before World War II and their subsequent development. Motion pictures are discussed in detail. The appendices include recommendations, catalogues, guides, and manuals dealing with some aspect of training aids.

344.   Philadelphia, Pennsylvania, Supervisor of Shipbuilding, "Wartime History: Supervisor of Shipbuilding, USN, Philadelphia, Pennsylvania, From Establishment November 1940, up to 1 September 1945." Shore Establishment, 1946. 15 pp. Index.

   This history contains a brief chronological account and summary of results. Much of the narrative is devoted to problem areas and how they were overcome.

345.   Philippine Sea Frontier, "Narrative History of the Philippine Sea Frontier." Sea Frontiers, 1945. 27 pp. Maps, illustrations.

The Philippine Sea Frontier, established in the summer of 1944, carried out such functions as the control of local naval defense forces and the protection of shipping through convoy and routing. This illustrated and well-organized narrative covers the period through the summer of 1945.

346.   PHOENIX (CL-46), Aviation Unit, "History of Aviation Unit, U.S.S. PHOENIX (CL-46)." Ships, 1945. 14 pp. Appendices.

This unit history consists of an operational chronology and appendices containing citations, awards, and a roster. Pacific operations of this ship from 7 December 1941 to 2 September 1945 are covered.

347.   Pineau, Roger, CAPT, "Japanese Carriers vs Land-Based Air in World War II." Individual Personnel, 1964. 38 pp.

In his study of Japanese air attacks on land-based targets in 1941-1942, Captain Pineau evaluates the effectiveness of carrier-based aircraft as opposed to land-based planes.

348.   PITTSBURGH (CA-72), Aviation Unit, "History of Aviation Unit, U.S.S. PITTSBURGH (CA-72)." Ships, 13 July 1945. 14 pp.

   This unit history covers the period from 1 August 1944 to 1 June 1945 in the Pacific Theater.

349.   Pittsburgh, Pennsylvania, Inspection District, "A Short History of the Pittsburgh Inspection District." Admin. Hist. Appen. Procurement and Material 5, n.d. 42 pp. Appendices.

   This is a well-written account of both the administrative and operational history of the district from its establishment in 1910 to early 1944.

350.   Pittsburgh, Pennsylvania, Supervisor of Shipbuilding, "Resume of History of Office of the Supervisor of Shipbuilding, USN, Neville Island, Pittsburgh, Pennsylvania." Shore Establishment, 1946. 13 pp.

   This history also contains accounts by assistant supervisors at the American Bridge Company, Ambridge, Pennsylvania, and Mt. Vernon and Ironton, Ohio. The accounts are in narrative form and discuss contracts awarded on a chronological basis.

351.   Pittsburgh University Historical Staff, Office of Naval Research, "The Administration of the Combat Information Center Program." 4 vols., Shore Establishment, 1952. 1460 pp.

A massive and detailed study, covering all aspects of the Combat Information Center development program.

352.   Pittsburgh University Historical Staff, Office of Naval Research, "The History of the United States Naval Research and Development in World War II." Shore Establishment,[1950.] 1650 pp.

This study is an extremely detailed work on naval technology during the World War II period. Most of the study is devoted to a comprehensive examination of technological and scientific advances made by the Navy during the war and immediate pre-war years. These are organized and discussed according to type (hull, ordnance, aircraft, radar, medicine, etc.). Also included are a review of naval technology since 1800, a brief administrative history of the navy organization for research and development, an account of the establishment of the Office of Naval Research in 1946, and a brief summary of research developments since World War II.

353.   Plymouth, Amphibious Receiving Base, "History of U.S. Naval Advanced Amphibious Receiving Base, Plymouth, Devon, England." Shore Establishment, 1945. 15 pp.

This report includes a chronological outline of important dates in the base's history and a narrative of activities at the base until its closing in 1945.

354.   Point Montara, California, Anti-Aircraft Training Center, "The Administrative History." Admin. Hist. Appen. 21 (13), n.d. 34 pp. Appendices.

This narrative and associated appendices furnish detailed information regarding the establishment and operations of the gunnery training program from January 1942 to late 1945.

355.   Pollock, Thomas F., CAPT, "Operation-Flight Gridiron: 27 April - 3 May 1942." Individual Personnel, 1963. 12 pp.

On 27 April 1942, two Navy PBY's departed Perth, Australia for Corregidor with orders to deliver medicine and supplies and bring out passengers from the beleaguered defenses. For this action, all flight personnel involved were awarded the Silver Star. Captain (then Lieutenant Junior Grade) Pollock was the pilot of the lead plane. This is a detailed and readable account of the mission.

356.   Port Hueneme, California, Anti-Aircraft Training Center, "Command History." Admin. Hist. Appen. 21 (12), 30 September 1945. 19 pp.

This is a short but detailed account of the Center's development from its establishment on 14 February 1944.

357.   Port Lyautey, Naval Air Station, "Brief History of Port Lyautey." Shore Establishment, 9 April 1951. 5 pp.

   This is a short outline history of the Naval Air Station, Port Lyautey, Morocco.

358.   PORTLAND (CA-33), Aviation Unit, "History of Aviation Unit, U.S.S. PORTLAND (CA-33)." Ships, 1 July 1945. 7 pp.

   This short unit history covers the period from 1933 to July 1945 and actions, such as Coral Sea, Midway, Santa Cruz, and Tarawa.

359.   Potts, Alfred B., LT, "Historical Narrative, Fiji Islands." Admin. Hist. Appen. SoPac. Admin. Hist. 34, 6 November 1945. 48 pp.

   This is a useful account of the relationship between the government of Fiji (a British Crown Colony), the New Zealand Armed Forces, and the resident American Armed Forces.

360.   Powell, Paulus P., RADM, "Camp Crocodile." Individual Personnel, 1950. 13 pp.

   During the greater part of the war, Rear Admiral (then Commodore) Powell served as Chief of Staff to Vice Admiral Theodore S. Wilkinson, Commander, Third Amphibious Force. His essay, "Camp Crocodile," (the name of Wilkinson's headquarters on Guadalcanal) is a character study of Admiral Wilkinson by a man who greatly admired him.

361.   Procurement and Material Office, Navy Department, "Administrative History of the Planning and Statistics Branch, Office of Procurement and Material, January 31, 1942 - February 14, 1945." Admin. Hist. Appen. Procurement and Material 3, 1 May 1945. 365 pp. Appendices.

This is a thorough account of the branch's origin and administration with numerous references and a detailed table of contents.

362.   Procurement and Material Office, Navy Department, "History of the Industry Cooperation Division." Admin. Hist. Appen. Procurement and Material 2, n. d. 180 pp. (approx). Appendices.

Thirteen pages discuss overall administrative responsibilities. Separate sections explain the role of ten regional offices, the scope of activities of the division, and the plan of operations on all levels of authority.

363.   Procurement and Material Office, Navy Department, "History of Surplus Property Disposal, World War I." Admin. Hist. Appen. Procurement and Material 20, n.d. 128 pp.

Based on a detailed analysis of Naval records, this fully-documented history explores the legal as well as fiscal implications of surplus disposal following World War I.

364.   Procurement and Material Office, Production Branch, Navy Department, "Naval History of the Current War." Admin. Hist. Appen. Procurement and Material 6, December 1944 - January 1945. 150 pp. (approx). Appendices.

   Rather than a comprehensive history of the branch, this document is comprised of several section histories of various length and quality. Sections included are: Chemicals, Food, Fuel, Machine Tools, Metals, Minerals, Production Scheduling, Rubber, Stockpile and Shipping, Textiles, and Transportation Equipment.

Q

365.   QUINCY (CA-71), Aviation Unit, "History of Aviation Unit, U.S.S. QUINCY (CA-71)." Ships, 1945. 3 pp.

   This brief unit history covers the period from October 1943 to September 1945, when QUINCY operated in the Atlantic and Pacific Theaters.

366.   Quincy, Massachusetts, Supervisor of Shipbuilding, "Wartime History of Supervisor of Shipbuilding, Bethlehem Steel Company, Quincy, Massachussetts." Shore Establishment, 1946. 12 pp. Appendices.

   This narrative stresses the chronological aspects of construction and the development of manpower resources.

R

367.   RALEIGH (CL-7), Aviation Unit, "History of Aviation Unit, U.S.S. RALEIGH (CL-7)." Ships, 8 May 1945. 2 pp.

   This brief unit history covers the period from August 1942 to January 1945 during which planes from RALEIGH spotted for the bombardment of Kiska Island and performed submarine patrol duty.

368.   RANGER (CV-4), "History of U.S.S. RANGER (CV-4)." Ships, 1945. 17 pp. Illustrations.

   This history covers the period from January 1942 to September 1945. RANGER served on Atlantic patrols and transport duty until being transferred to the Pacific Fleet in July 1945 as a qualification training ship for carrier pilots. This history was extracted from logs with gaps filled from memory. A two-page addendum describes in more detail the ship's role in the November 1942 North African landings.

369.   Ray, Clarence C., RADM, "Personal Recollection of Certain Events of the Battle of Midway." Individual Personnel, 1967. 17 pp.

   As the title suggests, this is a collection of anecdotes by Admiral Ray about his experiences on board YORKTOWN, which was sunk at Midway in June 1942.

370.   Recife, Brazil, Naval Air Facility, "Naval History." Admin. Hist. Appen. SOLANT 24 (17), n.d. 30 pp. Appendices, photographs.

   This history is composed primarily of subordinate office histories and mission outlines with only two pages of overall discussion. It covers the period from October 1943 to June 1945.

371.   Richard, Dorothy E., LCDR, "Hitler at Sea, 1942-1943." Individual Personnel, 1949. 24 pp.

   This graduate research paper traces all aspects of German Naval warfare in 1942-1943: the expansion of the war into American waters, the U-Boat campaign, scientific and technological developments, Admiral Raeder's Mediterranean strategy, and the internal political difficulties which culminated in Raeder's replacement by Doenitz and the abandonment of Germany's "big ship" Navy in favor of the U-Boats. Extensive footnotes are provided as well as a short bibliography.

372.   RICHMOND (CL-4), Aviation Unit, "History of Aviation Unit, U.S.S. RICHMOND (CL-4)." Ships, 1945. 4 pp. Appendices.

   This brief unit history covers the period from 7 December 1941 to 30 June 1945. RICHMOND's planes spotted for the bombardment of Attu and participated in patrol duty.

373.   Richmond, Virginia, Naval Training School (Diesel), "Administrative History of the Naval Training School (Diesel), Richmond, Virginia." Admin. Hist. Appen. 30 (1), 16 August 1945. 10 pp.

   The clearly written account cites the main accomplishments of this facility which offered training in the maintenance and operation of diesel engines.

374.		Rio de Janeiro, Brazil, Naval Operating Base, [Command History]. Admin. Hist. Appen. SOLANT 24 (18), n.d. 20 pp. Appendices, photographs.

   The skeletal outline with amplifying paragraphs covers 1 December 1942 to mid-1945.

375.		Risk, James C., LCDR, "Bases." Eighth Fleet, n.d. 150 pp.

   This is a rough draft, formerly entitled "The Bases of COMNAVNAW," which is Chapter VII of a larger, unidentified work. The study describes the establishment of naval shore bases in the Mediterranean, 1942-1945.

376.		Risk, James C., LCDR, "The History of Task Force 125, April 1945-January 1946." Naval Forces, 1946. 56 pp.

   The narrative deals with U.S. Naval forces in the Mediterranean during the closing days of the war in Europe. It is documented.

377.		Roskill, Stephen W., CAPT, RN, "Defense of Trade in World Wars I and II." Individual Personnel, 3 May 1968. 38 pp.

   In this speech before the Naval Historical Foundation, Captain Roskill, the Royal Navy's former official historian, presents a thorough examination of the defense of allied merchant shipping in the two World Wars and the state of naval readiness for these operations in the interwar period.

378.   Ruge, Friedrich, VADM, FGN, "Rommel and the 1944 Invasion." Lecture delivered at the Smithsonian Institution, Individual Personnel, 27 November 1964. 26 pp.

In November, 1943, Field Marshal Erwin Rommel was directed to inspect the defenses of Northwestern Europe as Commander, Army Group For Special Employment. Vice Admiral Ruge was assigned to his staff as Naval Advisor and remained with the Field Marshal until Rommel's death in October 1944. In his lecture, Ruge speaks as both Rommel's advisor and his friend. He gives a complete analysis of the German defenses along the Northern Wall.

379.   Russell Islands Naval Base, "First Narrative of the Russell Islands Naval Command." Shore Establishment, 1945. 83 pp. Appendices, maps, illustrations.

A thorough and well-documented report on the organization and functioning of the command from the American invasion through the Japanese surrender. This report also discusses the physical characteristics and the sociology of the area. The 16 appendices cover specialized aspects of the command's operations. Many excellent photographs are included.

S

380.   SABLE (IX-81), "History of U.S.S. SABLE (IX-81)." Ships, 12 May 1945. 3 pp.

SABLE was a training carrier commissioned on 8 May 1943. After conversion from S.S. GREATER BUFFALO, she was used on Lake Michigan. The period to 1 May 1945 is covered.

381.   Sackett, E. L., CAPT, "The CANOPUS." Individual Personnel, n.d. 26 pp.

An informal history of the submarine tender CANOPUS from the beginning of the war in the Pacific to her scuttling during the fall of Corregidor. It is a colorful account.

382.   ST. LOUIS (CL-49), Aviation Unit, "History of Aviation Unit, U.S.S. ST. LOUIS (CL-49)." Ships, 1945. 29 pp.

This unit history covers the period from September 1939 to September 1945. The history of this unit includes coverage on two of the cruiser's planes that attempted to fight off Japanese dive bombers at Pearl Harbor.

383.	Saipan Naval Base, "History of U.S. Naval Base, Navy No. 3245." Admin. Hist. Appen. 38 (16)(I), 15 October 1945. 70 pp. Appendices, photographs.

This history thoroughly examines the role of Saipan during World War II, from its early use as a staging area for Pacific invasions to its employment as a demobilization point at the termination of hostilities.

384.	Salber, Mary P., "History of the Supervisor of Shipbuilding, Tacoma, Washington." Shore Establishment, 1945. 153 pp. Appendices, illustrations.

This mainly covers the period 15 March 1945 through 14 August 1945, with emphasis on the activities and organization at Todd Pacific Shipyards, Tacoma. It is well illustrated with photographs of personnel and the shipyard, and includes organizational charts.

385.	Salvage Supervisor, New York, "A Short History of the Navy Salvage Service (Contract NOBS-36)." Shore Establishment, 1948. 215 pp. Appendices.

According to the history's letter of promulgation, the Navy Salvage Service was a "civilian-manned and managed organization, which under contract of the Navy Department, furnished offshore salvage protection to shipping... from December 1941 to May 1947." The study discusses the history of salvage operations before the war, preparations for wartime ship salvage, the contract with Merritt Chapman, and Scott, the establishment of the Salvage Service, the operation of the Service and its accomplishments, and the nature of salvage claims and awards.

386.   Samoan Defense Group, "United States Naval History of the Samoan Defense Group." Admin. Hist. Appen. SoPac. Admin. Hist. 84, 1 October 1945. 85 pp.

The text is divided into two major discussions: the naval bases, and a chronological summary of military activity through 1 October 1945. During the late stages of the Pacific War, the Samoan Defense Group was the largest area command in the South Pacific.

387.   Samoan Defense Group, "United States Naval History of Tutuila, American Samoa." Admin. Hist. Appen. SoPac Admin. Hist. 92, n.d. [approx. June 1945]. 162 pp.

The narrative recounts the Navy's role in American Samoa, the difficulties encountered, and the errors made and corrected.

388.   Samoan Defense Group, "United States Naval History of Western Samoa." Admin. Hist. Appen. SoPac. Admin. Hist. 97, n.d. [approx. September 1945]. 137 pp.

Concerned mainly with the Navy's involvement on Upolu, the text is divided into three sections: the advanced Naval Base as it existed on 1 August 1945, the arrival of American forces through 1 August 1945, and an analytical approach to political problems in Western Samoa.

389.   Sampson, New York, Naval Training Center, "U.S. Naval Training Center, Sampson, New York." Shore Establishment, 1945. 43 pp.

The narrative reviews the establishment, construction, and operation of the Navy Training Center and Recruit Training Command at Sampson, New York.

390.   San Clemente Island, California, Naval Auxiliary Air Station, "History and Development of CIC [Combat Information Center] Team Training Center, NAAS--San Clemente Island." Admin. Hist. Appen. 21 (18), 27 September 1945. 31 pp. Appendices.

The detailed and well-written history traces the command's mission from its inception in May 1943.

391.   SAN FRANCISCO (CA-38), Aviation Unit, "History of Aviation Unit, U.S.S. SAN FRANCISCO (CA-38)." Ships, 27 August 1945. 32 pp. Appendices.

This unit history covers the period from 8 December 1941 to 1 July 1945. It is well organized and contains much technical information about cruiser-based flying.

392.   San Francisco, California, Assistant Industrial Manager, "Wartime History of the Assistant Industrial Manager, USN, San Francisco, California." Shore Establishment, 22 March 1946. 97 pp. Index.

After brief accounts of the establishment and growth of this organization, the narrative focuses on accomplishments. Development and activities of certain sections such as the electronics department are described with special stress on problems that hampered operations.

393.   San Francisco, California, Naval Base, "History of Navy Chartered Transports of World War II." Shore Establishment, June 1946. 107 pp. Appendices.

In addition to a history of the subject, this document is concerned with the lessons learned. On an appendix data on all Navy chartered transports from 1943 to 1946 are tabulated.

394.   San Pedro, California, Shakedown Group, "Command History." Admin. Hist. Appen. 21 (10), n.d. 10 pp.

The short account of a training group charged with preparing crews to man new APA/AKA's and other large auxiliaries covers May 1944 to May 1945.

395.   Santa Cruz, Brazil, Naval Air Facility, /˜Command History˜/. Admin. Hist. Appen. 24 (33), n.d. 16 pp. Photographs.

The brief chronology, amplified by a detailed narrative, covers August 1942 to April 1945.

396.   SANTA FE (CL-60), Aviation Unit, "History of Aviation Unit, U.S.S. SANTA FE (CL-60)." Ships, 5 April 1945. 6 pp. Illustrations.

This unit history covers the period 21 December 1942-1 March 1945 in the Pacific Theater. A narrative of operations and list of citations and awards for this active unit are included. This history has numerous photographs.

397.   Santos, Brazil, Naval Operating Facility, "A History of the United States Naval Operating Facility, Santos, Brazil." Admin. Hist. Appen. 24 (19), 31 May 1945. 43 pp. Appendices, photographs.

Thoughtfully written and well documented, this study covers the transition of the Santos Naval Observer's Office from a temporary liaison role in March 1942 to a permanent support base.

398.   Sartin, Lea B., CAPT (MC), "Bilibid Letter Book, 1942." Hospital Corps Archives Memo 268-45, Shore Establishment, 1946. 69 letters.

The "Bilibid Letter Book" is a collection of papers relating to the organization and operation of Bilibid Prison Hospital, Manila in 1942. During this period, Captain Sartin was the medical officer in charge of the Naval Hospital Unit at Bilibid. These materials provide valuable insight into the experiences of prisoners of war with disease, malnutrition, inadequate facilities, and lack of supplies.

399.   Savannah, Georgia, Supervisor of Shipbuilding, "A Preliminary Outline History of the Activities of the Supervisor of Shipbuilding and Naval Inspector of Ordnance, USN, Savannah, Georgia, and its Various Assistant and Branch Offices for the Period of 20 April 1942 to 9 July 1945." Shore Establishment, 9 July 1945. 12 pp.

This preliminary outline is a critical analysis of these programs. Comments on labor relations are included.

400.   Savannah, Georgia, Supervisor of Shipbuilding, "Wartime History of the Supervisor of Shipbuilding, USN, Savannah, Georgia." Shore Establishment, 1946. 18 pp.

This activity was responsible for an area which stretched from Charleston, South Carolina to Jacksonville, Florida, and west to Tallahassee. This account includes details on the contracts and cost of each company.

401. Scientific Research and Development, Office of, "U.S. Rocket Ordnance; Development and Use in World War II." Shore Establishment, 1946. 57 pp. Illustrations.

    This account offers a review of the development and use of rockets and rocket-propelled weapons. The text is organized according to the use of the rockets (anti-submarine rockets, aircraft rockets,) and covers their use in both the Army and Navy.

402. Scott, Walter H., LCDR, "A Brief History of Transport Squadron Twelve Command." Individual Personnel, 1945. 87 pp.

    This well organized account covers landings at Saipan, Guam, Leyte and Lingayen Gulf during the period from 1943 to 1945. Biographical descriptions of officers and enlisted personnel assigned to the staff are included.

403. Scouting Force, U.S. Pacific Fleet, "Annual Report of Commander Scouting Force, U.S. Pacific Fleet, 1940 and 1941." Discontinued Commands, 1940, 1941. 107 pp.

    Organization, operations, communications, material, personnel, and inspections are discussed in these two reports.

404.   Seattle, Washington, APA Precommissioning School, "Command History." Admin. Hist. Appen. 21 (6), n.d. 19 pp.

   This well-written account, which covers June 1944 to March 1945, explains the duty, command relationships, physical description, staffing, curricula, and logistical support of the school, which was assigned the responsibility of training crews for newly constructed APA's.

405.   Seattle, Washington, Assistant to the Industrial Manager, "History of the Office of the Assistant to the Industrial Manager, USN, Seattle, Washington." Shore Establishment, 26 March 1946. 91 pp. Appendix.

   This account includes a brief chronological narrative but devotes most attention to organization and procedures. Unusually well organized, this history describes shipyards in the Seattle area as well as other facilities under supervision of the Assistant Industrial Manager.

406.   Service Force, Pacific, "Command History, Naval Personnel Office, Pacific." Admin. Hist. Appen. CinCPac/Poa Analytical Div. 37, n.d. 200 pp. (approx). Appendices, charts.

   This is a detailed analysis of the command's origin, mission, and activities from July 1944 to August 1945. This history includes not only a thorough overview, but a separate summary for each section as well.

407.   Service Force, Pacific, "A History of the Advanced Base Section." Type Commands, 1 October 1945. 125 pp.

A history of the Service Force group responsible for planning and organizing advanced bases on Japanese islands captured in the Central Pacific Area.

408.   Service Force, Pacific, "History of the Electronics Maintenance School." Admin. Hist. Appen. 38 (14) (A), September 1945. 135 pp. Appendices, charts, photographs.

This summary of the work of the main radar training activity in the Pacific during World War II includes course curricula in the appendices.

409.   Service Force, Pacific, "History of the Fleet Maintenance Office." Admin. Hist. Appen. CincPac/Poa Analytical Div. 21, 8 September 1945. 32 pp.

This history discusses the establishment, functions, initial organization, development, expansion, and duties, at the termination of hostilities, of the office.

410.   Service Force, Pacific, "History of Operations Office, Commander Service Force." Admin. Hist. Appen. 38 (9), n.d. 60 pp. Appendices.

This account traces the highlights of Pacific Fleet planning and management from the outbreak of the war to the beginning of demobilization.

411.   Service Force, Pacific, "History of the Radar Operators School." Admin. Hist. Appen. 38 (14) (A), n.d. (approx. October 1945). 90 pp. Appendices, photographs.

　　　　This history primarily consists of twelve appendices supporting the seven-page overview of operations of the school, which was erected at Pearl Harbor during World War II.

412.   Service Force, Pacific, "History of the Service Force Medical Office." Admin. Hist. Appen. 38 (5), n.d. 64 pp.

　　　　This survey of medical data includes material on the dental office and the headquarters dispensary at Pearl Harbor as well as general historical information.

413.   Service Force, Pacific, "Operation Roll-Up: The History of Surplus Property Disposal in the Pacific Ocean." Type Commands, 1948. 125 pp. Appendices.

　　　　This is both an administrative and operational history of the disposal and redistribution of material and equipment in the Pacific following World War II. Beginning on V-J Day, the task was not complete until 31 December 1947. This well-organized account, in addition to its table of contents, also has a good introduction and summary.

414.   Service Force, Seventh Fleet, "History of Service Force, U.S. Seventh Fleet." Type Commands, n.d. 94 pp. Illustrations.

An overall account that contains numerous photographs.

415.   Service Squadron Six, "Historical Report of Service Squadron Six." Type Commands, 1945. 7 pp. Tables, charts, annexes.

This narrative history of the unit describes operations from 25 November 1944 to 2 October 1945, during which time the unit participated in the Iwo Jima, Okinawa, and Japanese Home Island campaigns.

416.   Service Squadron, South Pacific, "History of Commander Service Squadron South Pacific, 7 December 1941 to 15 August 1945." Type Commands, 1946. 764 pp. Appendices, illustrations.

This is a thorough and scholarly command history. The account is well organized and contains illustrations, numerous appendices, a chronology, bibliography, and extensive footnotes. In addition to administrative history, this account includes interesting data on the physical characteristics of the area.

417.   Service Squadron, South Pacific Force, "Service Squadron South Pacific Force." Admin. Hist. Appen. 34 (1) (B), n.d. 10 pp.

   The readable survey highlights the early relationship between Service Force, Pacific Fleet and the completely new South Pacific command, SERVRONSOPAC, from April 1942 through late 1945.

418.   Seventh Amphibious Force, "History of the Seventh Amphibious Force." Type Commands, n. d. 63 pp. Illustrations.

   This general account of the command's operations in the Pacific during World War II is well illustrated and contains biographies of senior officers. Major operations included New Guinea, New Britain, Philippine Islands, Borneo, Korea, and China.

419.   Seventh Amphibious Force, "Seventh Amphibious Force Command History, 10 January 1943 - 23 December 1945." Type Commands, 1945. 109 pp. Maps, photographs, charts, tables.

   This history relates the unit's participation in Pacific amphibious operations. It was one of the basic sources for MacArthur's Amphibious Navy by Admiral Daniel E. Barbey (U.S. Naval Institute, Annapolis, 1969).

420.   Seventh Fleet, Intelligence Center, "Submarine Activities Connected with Guerrilla Organizations." Type Commands, 1945. 42 pp.

   This history is comprised of a brief resume of submarine operations supporting friendly guerrilla forces in the Philippines during the period 14 January 1943 to 23 January 1945. In addition to a summary sheet of the individual submarines and the numbers and types of missions, the account includes a series of brief, single-page summaries for 38 of the 41 missions conducted.

421.   Shaughnessy, William K., CDR, "Navy Participation in the Solution of United Nations Material Problems." Admin. Hist. Appen. Procurement and Material 22 (Tab 8 of LCDR Roy C. Hoffman's "Report on Lend-Lease Activities in the Department of the Navy Before and During World War II."), 29 March 1946. 104 pp. Appendices.

   This is a documented and well-organized history of all aspects of the Navy's role which included screening foreign military procurement within the U.S., transfer of equipment to allied countries, and providing transportation to fit their needs. See also entry 199.

422.   Shepherd, George C., Jr., CDR, "War History, Area Petroleum Office Service Force, U.S. Pacific Fleet." Admin. Hist. Appen. 38 (15) (A), December 1945. 120 pp. Appendices, charts.

   This contains an outline of this office's mission and an explanation of the ample appendices.

423.   Shields, Henry S., CAPT., USAF, "A Historical Survey of the United States Naval Attaches in Russia: 1904-1941." Individual Personnel, 1970. 83 pp. Appendices, bibliography.

In this M.A. thesis, Captain Shields has broken the history of U.S. naval attaches in Russia into six chronological areas. The author used naval attache reports as well as other primary sources in his research.

424.   Sitterson, J. Carlyle, "Aircraft Production Policies Under the National Defense Advisory Commission and Office of Production Management: May 1940 to December 1941." Admin. Hist. Appen. War Admin., 30 May 1946. 168 pp. Appendices.

This study traces the effect of wartime requirements on aircraft production programs. Among the subjects covered are: coordinating the needs of the Army, Navy, and foreign governments, who would all draw on the same production facilities; reconciling the civilian demand for commercial transports with the military version of the same aircraft; and instilling a mass production philosophy among aircraft manufacturers.

425.   Sixth Marine Division, Intelligence Section, "The Sixth Marine Division on Okinawa Shima." USMC, 1 August 1945. 64 pp. Maps, illustrations.

This is a summary of Okinawa operations written for the benefit of those to be involved in future operations on Japanese soil. A 21-day diary of a dead Japanese soldier opposing the Okinawa invasion is included.

426.   Smith, Richard K., LT, "An Inventory of U.S. Navy Airships With Miscellaneous Characteristics, Performance and Contract Data, 1916 -1961." Individual Personnel, n.d. 138 pp.

As the title suggests, the study is a compilation of significant information on historical and technological aspects of the Navy's airships. In addition to statistical tables, chronological narratives are provided for each of the rigid airships and for each type of non-rigid blimp serving in the Navy.

427.   SOUTH DAKOTA (BB-57), Aviation Unit, "History of Aviation Unit, U.S.S. SOUTH DAKOTA (BB-57)." Ships, 1945. 8 pp. Appendices.

This unit history covers the period 2 May 1942 to 1 April 1945 in the Pacific Theater.

428.   South Pacific Aircraft Training Unit, "History of the South Pacific Aircraft Training Unit, Espiritu Santo." Admin. Hist. Appen. 34 (2), April 1945. 30 pp. Appendices, photographs.

Established in late 1943, SPATU's mission was the training of SOPAC aviation units to assure air superiority in the final stages of the war in the Pacific. The history is largely a month-by-month summary of the training schedule.

429.   South Pacific Area and Forces, "History of New Zealand During World War II." Admin. Hist. Appen. 34 (16) - 34 (16) (M), n.d. 567 pp.

   This extensive three-part study of World War II's impact on manpower, sea frontier organization, and shipbuilding and ship repair facilities is based on the records of the New Zealand Chief War Archivist.

430.   South Pacific Area and Forces, "New Caledonia." Admin. Hist. Appen. 34 (10) - 34 (10) (A), n.d. 65 pp. Appendices, charts.

   A summary of the military uses of this French possession during World War II includes a report on post-war usage of New Caledonia prepared for the House of Representatives Naval Affairs Committee in the appendices.

431.   South Pacific Area and Forces, Photographic and Reproduction Unit, "An Informal History of the COMSOPAC Photographic and Reproduction Unit." Shore Establishment, 15 September 1945. 70 pp. Appendices, illustrations.

   The narrative account, based on individual recollections assembled from the unit's personnel files, contains numerous photographs, charts, forms, manuals, and correspondence of general interest.

432.   South Pacific Area and Forces, "Report on Franco-American Relationship in New Caledonia." Admin. Hist. Appen. 34 (10) (C), n.d. 70 pp. Appendices.

   This is an excellent overview of relationships, which at times were strained, between the French, New Caledonians, and U.S. representatives. New Caledonia was an important U.S. supply base during operations in the Pacific Theater.

433.   Spalding, P. E., et al., "The War Record of Civilian and Industrial Hawaii." Individual Personnel, 1945. 127 pp.

   This study was prepared for the Joint Congressional Committee to Investigate the Pearl Harbor attack as a documentary history of the assistance extended to the armed forces by the civilian and business communities of Hawaii. It primarily consists of a compilation of documents with only a brief narrative.

434.   Stecher, Robert W., LT, "History of the U.S.S. TREPANG (SS-412)." Ships, 1945. 16 pp.

   This is the command history of a submarine which sank 15 ships in the Pacific. It is a spirited account of a unit commissioned May 1944 and decommissioned June 1946.

435.   Sternhell, Charles M. and Alan M. Thorndike, "Antisubmarine Warfare in World War II: OEG Report No. 51." CNO, 1946. 193 pp. Appendices, maps, illustrations, index.

   This comprehensive study is divided into two broad categories: "History of Antisubmarine Operations." and "Antisubmarine Measures and Their Effectiveness." It contains an excellent glossary.

436.   Stockly, Louise T., "History of the Naval Reserve Midshipman's School (WR), Northampton, Mass." Admin. Hist. Appen. 15 (OO), 19 December 1945. 98 pp.

   A thorough work providing a comprehensive overview of the WAVE officer training school at Smith College during World War II.

437.   Stockton, James R., CAPT, USMC, "The Sixth Marine Division." USMC, 1945. 19 pp. Appendices, maps, illustrations.

   This is a brief outline history of the last of the famous Marine divisions of World War II. Appendices contain a list of command and staff personnel.

438.   Stump, Felix B., ADM, "An Evening With ADM Felix B. Stump." Individual Personnel, 1967. 32 pp.

This contains recollections and opinions of Admiral Stump, who served as commanding officer of LEXINGTON during part of World War II, and as Commander-in-Chief Pacific and U.S. Pacific Fleet in the early 1950's.

439.   Submarine Escape Committee, "Submarine Escapes - Past and Present." Appendix-1 to Report of Submarine Escape Committee, Shore Establishment, 1947. 32 pp.

The study recounts many instances of escapes from sunken submarines beginning with the German submarine U-3 which sank in Kiel before 1914. Some accounts are quite lengthy, drawing much of their information from the survivors themselves, while some are fairly brief.

440.   Submarine Force, Atlantic Fleet, "Administrative History of Commander, Submarines, Atlantic Fleet." Type Commands, 1945. 17 pp.

Written in narrative form, this history deals with the wartime administration and support of the Atlantic Fleet Submarine Force. Included are data on training, staff organization, and vessel dispositions.

441.   Submarine Force, Pacific, "The History of Submarine Warfare in the Pacific." Type Commands, n.d. 275 pp.

   This volume appears to be an initial draft of a larger and more complete work. Essentially, it is a narrative of selected patrols based on the reports of various submarines. The account ends with November 1943.

442.   Submarine Force, Pacific Fleet, "Submarine Operational History World War II." 4 vols., Type Commands, 14 May 1947. Appendices, maps, illustrations, index.

   This extensive account is based primarily on over 1500 submarine war patrol reports received by the Pacific Submarine Force. The narrative deals almost exclusively with the Pacific area and is primarily operational in nature. This history served as a major source for Theodore Roscoe's <u>United States Submarine Operations in World War II</u> (U.S. Naval Institute, 1949).

443.   [Submarine Squadron 50], "The Work of U.S. SUBRON Fifty in European Waters, 1942 - 43." Type Commands, 1948. 13 pp. Maps.

   This narrative was prepared from Admiralty and Axis documents. The account describes Submarine Squadron Fifty's operations in the Bay of Biscay under control of the British Admiralty.

444.   Submarines, Scouting Force, U.S. Pacific Fleet, "Annual Report of the Commander, Scouting Force, U.S. Pacific Fleet, FY 1941." Discontinued Commands, 1941. 12 pp.

Organization, operations and training, material, personnel, and inspections are discussed.

445.   Sullivan, William A., COMO, "Ship Salvage and Harbor Clearance." Individual Personnel, 4 December 1947. 41 pp.

This lecture by Commodore Sullivan, at the Naval War College, is a critical examination of American salvage organization and procedures during World War II. The lecture discusses at length the organization of an individual harbor salvage group and the harbor clearance work performed in Naples Harbor.

446.   Supplies and Accounts, Bureau, Historical Section, "First Draft of Administrative History of Supply Corps Procurement in World War II (Interim Report)." Shore Establishment, 1945. 223 pp.

The Bureau's history is a thorough and informative study of Navy procurement practices and policies before and during World War II. Largely devoid of technical terminology and abbreviations, the report explains procurement methods and problems in familiar terms. A concise history of the Supply Corps is included, although it is not documented.

447.   Supplies and Accounts, Bureau, "Summary of the Supply System for BUSANDA Materials Continental United States and Pacific Ocean Areas." Shore Establishment, April 1945. 31 pp.

   This is a description of the naval supply system, with stress on ship's store stock, clothing and small stores, provisions, and petroleum products.

448.   Swarthout, Rassele E., CDR (CEC), "Activities of the Bureau of Yards and Docks in the European Theater of Operations, 1941-1945." Individual Personnel, n.d. 67 pp.

   In his introduction, Commander Swarthout divides the wartime activity of the Bureau of Yards and Docks (including the Civil Engineering Corps and the Construction Battalions) into three phases: the establishment of American Naval facilities in Great Britain, largely completed by mid-1943; the preparation for the assult on the continent; and the support of the Allied Invasion Force in Europe. It appears that the final section of the manuscript, covering some of phase two and all of phase three, has been lost. Nevertheless, the available text provides a lengthy examination of the establishment of the Navy's bases in Londonderry, Rosneath, Lough Erne, and Loch Ryan. Topics covered include command activities, liaison with British and U.S. Army officials, civilian contracts, and the construction and functions of the four bases.

449.   Swift, Roy L., CDR, "History of USS BLOCK ISLAND (CVE's 21 and 106)." Ships, 1968. 78 pp.

Detailed history of CVE-21, which was sunk in the Atlantic on 29 May 1944, and CVE-106, which continued the war in the Pacific with much of the same crew. The CVE-21 was an especially successful anti-submarine carrier.

T

450.   Talbot, Melvin F., CDR, "The Logistics of the Eighth Fleet and Commander U.S. Naval Forces Northwest African Waters." Fleets, 1945. 77 pp.

This history provides an excellent, though undocumented, history of the logistics of the Eighth Fleet in the Mediterranean from 1942 to 1945. The logistical planning behind the landings at Casablanca, Oran, and Algiers is highlighted.

451.	Tampa, Florida, Supervisor of Shipbuilding, "Wartime History of the Office of Supervisor of Shipbuilding, USN, Tampa, Florida." Shore Establishment, 1945. 47 pp. Appendices, maps, illustrations, index.

   Emphasis is given to the organization and procedures used by the Tampa Shipbuilding Company. Information on personnel and plant values are included, as is an excellent section on labor relations.

452.	Tamura, Kyuzo, "History of Japanese Minesweeping, 1937-1947." Individual Personnel, 1948. 66 pp. Appendices.

   Although this history covers a 10-year period, beginning with the moored minesweeping operations in the Yangtze River in 1937 and extending through World War II, the account dwells primarily on postwar operations. After the war, American and Japanese Naval Forces combined to clear the waters around Japan and China of more than 15,000 mines laid by both sides during the war. The effectively organized narrative is supported by an abundance of mine-disposal statistics, as well as explanatory diagrams of minesweeping gear and vessels used in the operations.

453.   Task Force 24, "The History of Task Force 24."
Task Forces, 1942. 150 pp.

    This command history was prepared sometime in
early 1942. It describes in detail the administrative organization and planning of the U.S.
Escorts protecting convoys (Task Force 24) in the
North Atlantic during 1941. Development of bases
in Newfoundland, Iceland, and Greenland is also
described. Actual operations, such as the Greer
and Kearney incidents, are mentioned, but are not
the central theme.

454.   Task Group 96.1, Shore-Based Air Force,
Marshalls-Gilberts Area, "Command History." Admin.
Hist. Appen. 18E, 30 August 1945. 97 pp. Appendices.

    The narrative traces the activities of Naval
and Marine air squadrons assigned to this area
during World War II. Specific units included VMSB-
331, VMB-613, VMF-111, VS-66, and VPB-144.

455.   Tate, E. Mowbray, "U. S. Gunboats on the
Yangtze: History and Political Aspects, 1842-1922."
Individual Personnel, 1965. 14 pp.

    Professor Tate's paper, presented to the Midwest Conference on Asian Affairs, examines American
diplomatic relations with China from 1842 and the
use of American Naval Gunboats to protect American
interests and American citizens in the Yangtze
Valley--a policy which grew out of an interpretation of the most-favored clauses in the several
treaties concluded with the Chinese. Events following the reorganization of the Yangtze Patrol in
1920, including the Panay Incident of 1937, are
briefly mentioned. Documentation includes extensive footnotes and a solid bibliography.

456.   Taylor, Edwin J., Jr., RADM, "Memoirs 1941-1946." Individual Personnel, 1946. 29 pp.

   The author's wartime duties included tours on board ALABAMA and as Executive Officer on board SOUTH DAKOTA with action at Leyte Gulf and the Philippine Sea.

457.   Tenth Fleet, "History of the Anti-Submarine Measures Division of Tenth Fleet." Fleets, n.d. 67 pp.

   The history is concerned with the efforts of the Tenth Fleet, and additionally traces developments from 1941 in anti-submarine measures, organization, training, tactical doctrine, and detection devices that made possible the counteroffensive against German submarines in the summer of 1943. The history continues to discuss changes following the establishment of the Tenth Fleet in May 1943 to its disestablishment in 1945, and ends with a brief summary of prospects for anti-submarine warfare in the future. Coverage of actual combat operations is limited.

458.   Thacker, Joel D., "The First Marine Division, 1941-1945." USMC, n.d. 34 pp.

   This is a brief outline history of the Division's participation in such Pacific campaigns as Tulagi, Guadalcanal, New Britain, Peleliu, and Okinawa.

459.   Thacker, Joel D., "Marine Corps Aviation on Aircraft Carriers (Prior to World War II)." USMC, n.d. 4 pp.

This is a very brief outline history of the period between World War I and World War II.

460.   Thacker, Joel D., "Stand, Gentlemen, He Served on Samar." USMC, March 1945. 5 pp.

This is a short history of the Marine campaign on Samar against the Philippine insurgents in 1901.

461.   Thacker, Joel D., "The Torpedo Plane." USMC, March 1945. 7 pp.

This is a brief history of the torpedo plane before and during World War II.

462.   Tiburon, California, Floating Drydock Shakedown Group and Floating Drydock Training Center, "Command History." Admin. Hist. Appen. 21 (9), n.d. 7 pp.

The short but detailed accounting of the methods for training crews in the utilization of a mobile drydock facility covers the period December 1943 to December 1944.

463.		Tinian, Marianas, Mine Assembly Depot Number Four, "Administrative History and Phase Analysis of Mine Assembly Depot Number 4." Shore Establishment, 11 August 1945. 12 pp. Illustrations.

This very brief but well organized and detailed history contains graphs on mine production for 1945.

464.		Tinian Naval Base, Mariana Islands, "History of United States Naval Base, Tinian, Marianas Islands." Admin. Hist. Appen. 38 (16) (G), 11 October 1945. 58 pp. Appendices, charts, photographs.

A useful summary of the role played by the Naval base which supported B-29 operations against the Japanese home islands in the latter stages of World War II.

465.		Tongatabu Advanced Naval Base, "History of Tongatabu." Shore Establishment, 1945. 228 pp. Appendices, illustrations.

A detailed history of the island from 1939 through 1945 discusses the U.S. base and U.S. relations with Tongatabu and New Zealand.

466.   Transport Division 1, "Historical Record, Transport Division One." Type Commands, n.d. 29 pp.

   Over half of this report is devoted to a chronology of operations during 1944-1945 in the area of the Amphibious Training Base, Coronado, California.

467.   Transport Division 45, "History of Transport Division Forty-Five." Type Commands, 1945. 9 pp.

   This is a brief report of this Division's operations during 1944-1945 in the Pacific Theater, including Iwo Jima, Okinawa, and Japan.

468.   Transport Division 59, "Staff Gangway." Type Commands, 1945. 41 pp.

   This history covers the period 22 November 1944 to 25 December 1945. Photographs are included in this well-organized narrative. The highlight is the landing at Lingayen Gulf. The transportation of Chinese Troops at the end of the war is covered.

469.   Transport Division 60, "History of Commander, Transport Division Sixty, Amphibious Forces, U.S. Pacific Fleet." Type Commands, n.d. 19 pp.

   This is a brief discussion of the operations of this Division in 1945 on Eniwetok, Okinawa, the Marianas, and Japan.

470.   Transport Division 103, "History of Transport Division One Hundred-Three." Type Commands, n.d. 7 pp.

   This is a brief recounting of operations of this Division during 1944-1945 in the area of New Guinea, Leyte Gulf, Mindoro, Luzon, Mindanao, and Balikpapan.

471.   Transport Division 105, "History of Transport Division One Hundred-Five." Type Commands, n.d. 9 pp.

   This is a brief report of operations of this Division during 1945 on Leyte, Iwo Jima, Okinawa, Guam, and Japan.

472.   Transport Squadron 11, "Transport Squadron Eleven, Including Transport Divisions Twenty and Twenty-One." Type Commands, n.d. 9 pp.

   An extremely brief account covering the period of 1943-1945, with mention of operations at Makin Atoll, Eniwetok, Saipan, Guadalcanal, Guam, Manus, Leyte, New Guinea, and Iwo Jima.

473.   Transport Squadron 14, "Command History of Transport Squadron Fourteen, United States Fleet, September 3, 1943 to August 14, 1945." Type Commands, n.d. 36 pp.

   This history relates the operations of this Pacific Squadron in such invasions as Saipan, Tinian Island, Yap, Manus, Luzon, and Okinawa.

474.   Transport Squadron 16, "Transport Squadron Sixteen." Type Commands, n.d. 28 pp.

   This Squadron was formed late in the war. It participated in the Okinawa Landings. Three pages are devoted to a historical narrative and the remainder to staff instructions.

475.   Transport Squadron 19, "Transport Squadron Nineteen, Amphibious Forces, Pacific Fleet." Type Commands, n.d. 10 pp.

   This history is a chronological listing of the major events from the Squadron's formation in January 1945 through its participation at Okinawa.

476.   Transport Squadron 20, "Transport Squadron Twenty." Type Commands, n.d. 18 pp.

   This report is made up mostly of chronological listings of events during 1944-1945 in the area of New Caledonia, Guadalcanal, Luzon, Manus Island, Leyte Gulf, Iwo Jima, and Eniwetok.

477.   Transport Squadron 21, "Transport Squadron Twenty-One." Type Commands, n.d. 5 pp.

   Along with a narrative of operations in 1945 in the area of Eniwetok, Ulithi, and Okinawa, this account includes staff instructions and a staff roster.

478.	Transport Squadron 22, "Transport Squadron Twenty-Two." Type Commands, n.d. 4 pp.

    This history relates operations of the squadron during 1945, especially in the Hawaiian area.

479.	Transport Squadron 23, "Transport Squadron Twenty-Three." Type Commands, n.d. 2 pp.

    This is a very brief account. Transport Squadron 23 engaged in no combat.

480.	Transport Squadron 24, "Transport Squadron Twenty-Four." Type Commands, n.d. 2 pp.

    This report includes staff instructions and a brief chronology of events during June - August 1945 while the unit was engaged in refresher training off San Diego and planning in Hawaii for the projected invasion of Japan.

481	Treasure Island, California, Naval Training School, "History of Establishment and Operation Naval Training School (Electronic Material), Treasure Island, San Francisco, California." Type Commands, 1948. 26 pp.

    This condensed historical narrative covers the formative period of this training school, 1941-1945. The account emphasizes communication training. Comments on the beginnings of radar and electronics warfare are indicated. Pertinent appendices are included, dealing with organization, cost, and land surveys.

482. Treasure Island, California, Precommissioning Training Center, "History of Precommissioning Training Center." Admin. Hist. Appen. 21 (7), 14 August 1945. 200 pp. Appendices.

A brief accounting of one of several west coast training activities charged with the preparation of crews to operate new ships. The bulk of the report is made up of training exhibits.

483. Tredinnick, Frank A., Jr. and Harrison L. Bennett, "An Administrative History of PT's in World War II." Individual Personnel, 1946. 222 pp. Appendices, illustrations.

In addition to serving as an administrative history of Motor Torpedo Boat organization in World War II, this history provides an extensive examination of the development of Motor Torpedo Boats in Europe in the early Twentieth Century and their adoption by the U.S. Navy in the late 1930's. Particular attention is devoted to the trial-and-error evolution of the motor torpedo boat design. The text is supported by a good selection of photographs and extensive documentation.

484. TRENTON (CL-11), Aviation Unit, "History of Aviation Unit, TRENTON (CL-11)." Ships, 1945. 8 pp.

This unit history covers 1 December 1941 - 30 June 1945 in the Pacific Theater.

485.   Tucker, B. C., LCDR, "War History-U. S. Naval Detachment-Navy 316-Advance Base Idle." Shore Establishment, April 1944. 8 pp.

Lieutenant Commander Tucker's account is a personal record of the accomplishments of Navy 316, the Navy Detachment assigned to the Army-Navy Composite Task Force on Ascension Island. His coverage of the establishment of the base is quite complete. Information on life on this remote island outpost is included.

486.   Tulagi Advanced Naval Base, "History of Advanced Naval Base, Tulagi, British Solomon Islands." Shore Establishment, 1 August 1945. 216 pp. Appendices.

This account traces the development of the base during World War II from its early use as a staging and supply point to its final mission as a minor fueling depot and fleet anchorage.

487.   Twentieth Air Force, "Starvation." Air Force, 1945. 56 pp. Maps, illustrations.

This account depicts the B-29 strategic blockade of the Japanese Empire. Ten annexes contain technical details.

U

488. Ulithi Atoll Commander, "Preliminary Arrangements for Surrender of Japanese Held Islands of Yap, Sorol, and Fauripik." Naval Forces, August 1945. 11 pp.

   This compendium of letters and dispatches pertaining to the formal surrender arrangements for these islands in the Carolines contains both plans and a report of actual surrender, as well as a Japanese-language version of the surrender document.

489. Ulithi Naval Base, "Ulithi Base History." Shore Establishment, 1945. 8 pp. Appendices.

   A short command history of this base in the Western Carolines.

490. Underwater Demolition Teams 1 and 2, "History of Underwater Demolition Teams 1 and 2." Shore Establishment, 1947. 7 pp.

   An account of UDT operations in the Tarawa and Marshall Campaigns.

491.   Underwater Demolition Team 3, "History of Underwater Demolition Team 3." Shore Establishment, 1945. 15 pp.

This account of UDT 3's formation and participation in the Marianas, Leyte, and Japanese Occupation campaigns includes lists of personnel.

492.   Underwater Demolition Team 4, "History of Underwater Demolition Team 4." Shore Establishment, n.d. 6 pp. Appendix.

The brief description of this unit's history from March 1944 - October 1945, including operations at Guam, Leyte Gulf, and Okinawa, contains a list of officers and men in the appendix.

493.   Underwater Demolition Team 5, "History of Underwater Demolition Team 5." Shore Establishment, n.d. 18 pp. Appendix.

The brief history of this unit from January 1944 - October 1945 includes operations in Saipan, Roi Namur, Tinian, Yap, Marcus, Luzon, and Japan and contains a muster list of officers and men in the appendix.

494.   Underwater Demolition Team 6, "History of Underwater Demolition Team 6." Shore Establishment, n.d. 4 pp. Appendix.

The brief history of this unit, from May 1944 - November 1945, which operated in the Saipan, Guam, Tinian, Peleliu, and Leyte Gulf areas, contains a muster list of officers and men in the appendix.

495.	Underwater Demolition Team 7, "History of Underwater Demolition Team 7." Shore Establishment, n.d. 16 pp. Appendix.

The history of this unit from April 1944 - October 1945 includes operations at Saipan, Tinian, Manus, Okinawa, and Japan. A muster list of officers and men of this unit is included.

496.	Underwater Demolition Team 8, "History of Underwater Demolition Team 8." Shore Establishment, n.d. 12 pp. Appendix.

The history, which covers the period of 2 June 1944 - 12 November 1945, discusses the team's operations at Anguar, Peleliu, Leyte Gulf, Bougainville, and Lingayen Gulf. A muster list of officers and men is included.

497.	Underwater Demolition Team 9, "History of Underwater Demolition Team 9." Shore Establishment, n.d. 9 pp. Appendix.

This brief history, covering May 1944 - November 1945, discusses operations at Leyte, Lingayen, and Jinsen, Korea. An appendix contains a muster list of officers.

498.	Underwater Demolition Team 10, "History of Underwater Demolition Team 10." Shore Establishment, n.d. 5 pp. Appendix.

The brief history of this unit from June 1944 - February 1946 discusses operations at Anguar, Ulithi, Leyte Gulf, and Subic Bay. The appendix contains a muster list of officers and men.

499.   Underwater Demolition Team 12, "History of Underwater Demolition Team 12." Shore Establishment, n.d. 6 pp. Appendix.

This history covers the period September 1944 - November 1945 and discusses operations at Iwo Jima, Okinawa, and Jinsen, Korea. The appendix contains names of silver and bronze star recipients.

500.   Underwater Demolition Team 13, "History of Underwater Demolition Team 13." Shore Establishment, n.d. 4 pp. Appendix.

This brief history covers the period July 1944 - November 1945 and discusses operations at Iwo Jima and Okinawa. The appendix contains a roster of officers and men.

501.   Underwater Demolition Team 14, "History of Underwater Demolition Team 14." Shore Establishment, n.d. 3 pp. Appendix.

This brief history covers the period from September 1944 to October 1945 when the unit engaged in operations at Lingayen, Iwo Jima, and Okinawa. The appendix includes a roster of officers and men.

502.   Underwater Demolition Team 16, "History of Underwater Demolition Team 16." Shore Establishment, n.d. 3 pp. Appendix.

This history covers the period September 1944 - October 1945. Operations at Okinawa are discussed. The appendix contains a roster of officers and men.

503.   Underwater Demolition Team 17, "History of Underwater Demolition Team 17." Shore Establishment, n.d. 7 pp. Appendix.

The period October 1944 - October 1945 is covered during which the unit was involved in operations at Okinawa and the Wakayama beaches in Japan. The appendix contains a roster of officers and enlisted men.

504.   Underwater Demolition Team 18, "History of Underwater Demolition Team 18." Shore Establishment, n.d. 8 pp. Appendix.

The period November 1944 - November 1945 is discussed in this report, when the unit took part in operations at Balikpapan in Borneo and in the Tokyo Bay Area. The appendix contains a roster of officers and men.

505.   Underwater Demolition Team 19, "History of Underwater Demolition Team 19." Shore Establishment, n.d. 3 pp. Appendix.

This short history covers the period from September 1944 to October 1945, during which the unit participated in operations at Okinawa. The appendix contains a list of officers and men.

506.   Underwater Demolition Team 20, "History of Underwater Demolition Team 20." Shore Establishment, n.d. 2 pp. Appendix.

This brief history covers operations from September 1944 to November 1945, including the surrender of the city of Hakodate, Japan. The appendix contains a roster of officers and men.

507.   Underwater Demolition Team 23, "History of Underwater Demolition Team 23." Shore Establishment, n.d. 2 pp. Appendix.

   December 1944 - November 1945 is the period covered in this brief history. Operations were at Jinsen, Korea and at Okinawa. The appendix contains the names of officers and men.

508.   Underwater Demolition Team 25, "History of Underwater Demolition Team 25." Shore Establishment, n.d. 2 pp. Appendix.

   This brief history covers the period from October 1944 to November 1945 when the team participated in operations off the coast of Yokosuka and Yokohama, Japan. The appendix contains a list of officers and men.

509.   Underwater Demolition Team 27, "History of Underwater Demolition Team 27." Shore Establishment, n.d. 13 pp. Appendices.

   This history covers the period from February to October 1945, during which the unit was engaged in training at Fort Pierce, Florida, and Maui, Hawaiian Islands. A roster of officers and men plus a chronology of events are included.

510.   Underwater Demolition Team 30, "History of Underwater Demolition Team 30." Shore Establishment, n.d. 1 p. Appendix.

   The brief history of this unit covers the period April - October 1945 during which the unit was undergoing training. The appendix contains a roster of officers and men.

511.   Underwater Demolition Team, Pacific Fleet, "History of Commander Underwater Demolition Teams and Underwater Demolition Flotilla, Amphibious Forces, Pacific Fleet." Shore Establishment, n.d. 6 pp.

   This is a short account of the origin of this command. It is followed by histories of each team.

512.   United Kingdom Amphibious Bases, "A History of The United States Naval Bases in the United Kingdom." Shore Establishment, 1 November 1944. 271 pp. Illustrations.

   This history is divided into two parts: a group of staff department histories and base histories. The latter, which are written by base officers with an emphasis on human interest, are of varying length, well illustrated, and written in a frequently colorful style.

513.   United States Fleet, Commander-in-Chief, "Annual Reports of the Commander-in-Chief, U.S. Fleet 1923-1940." Discontinued Commands, 1923-1940. 1169 pp.

   This series of individually published annual reports gives detailed accounts of fleet activities, readiness, training, and personnel.

514.	United States Fleet, Commander-in-Chief, "Battle Experiences." 26 vols., CNO, 1943-1945. 3022 pp.

    These bulletins were intended to provide officers with reliable information concerning actual war experience so that the lessons learned during the war might be put to good advantage. The following titles are included:

    #1   "Battle Experience from Pearl Harbor to Midway," December 1941 - June 1942, including Makin Island Raid 17-18 August 1942.

    #2   "Battle Experience Solomon Islands Actions," August - September 1942, including Bombardment of Kiska 7 August 1942.

    #3   "Battle Experience Solomon Islands Actions," October 1942.

    #4   "Battle Experience Solomon Islands Actions," November 1942.

    #5   "Battle Experience Solomon Islands Actions," December 1942 - January 1943.

    #6   "Battle Experience, Solomon Islands and Alaskan Actions," January - February 1943.

    #7   "Battle Experience, Solomon Islands and Alaskan Actions," March 1943.

#8 "Battle Experience Solomon Islands and Alaskan Areas Bombardments," May and July 1943.

#9 "Battle Experience, Assault and Occupation of Attu Island," May 1943.

#10 "Battle Experience Naval Operations, Solomon Islands Area." 30 June - 12 July 1943.

#11 "Battle Experience Naval Operations Solomon Islands Area, 12 July - 10 August 1943.

#12 "Battle Experience, Solomon Islands and Alaskan Areas," July - October 1943.

#13 "Battle Experience, Bombardment of Wake Island," 5 and 6 October 1943.

#14 "Battle Experience Naval Operations South and Southwest Pacific Ocean Areas," 6 October - 2 November 1943.

#15 "Battle Experience, Supporting Operations Before and During the Occupation of the Gilbert Islands," November 1943.

#16 "Battle Experience, Battle Off Cape St. George, New Ireland," 24-25 November 1943.

#17 "Battle Experience, Supporting Operations for the Occupation of the Marshall Islands, including Eniwetok," February 1944.

#18 "Battle Experience, Battleship, Cruiser, and Destroyer Sweep Around Truk, 16-17 February 1944. Bombardments of Satawan and Ponape 30 April - 1 May 1944."

#19 "Battle Experience, Supporting Operations for the Invasion of Northern France," June 1944.

#20 "Battle Experience, Supporting Operations for the Capture of the Marianas Islands (Saipan, Guam, and Tinian)," June - August 1944.

#21 "Battle Experience, Night Action and Subsequent Bombardment of Chichi Jima and Ani Jima, Bonin Islands," 4-5 August 1944.
"Destruction of Japanese Convoy off Bislig Bay," 9 September 1944.
"Supporting Operations for the Occupation of Palau and Ulithi," September - October 1944.

#22 "Battle Experience, Battle for Leyte Gulf: A) Battle of Surigao Strait, B) Battle off Samar, C) Battle off Cape Engano," 23-27 October 1944.

#23 "Battle Experience, Bombardments of Iwo Jima, November 1944 - January 1945. Third Fleet Operations in Support of Central Luzon Landings, including the South China Sea Sweep 30 December 1944 - 23 January 1945."

#24 "Battle Experience, Radar Pickets and Methods of Combatting Suicide Attacks off Okinawa," March - May 1945.

#25 "Battle Experience, Encountering Typhoons or Storms," June -August 1945.

#26 "Battle Experience, Final Opinions of Units of the Pacific Fleet Off the Shores of Japan," July - August 1945.

515. United States Fleet, Commander-in-Chief, "Historical Summary - December 7, 1941 to December 7, 1942." CNO, n.d. 17 pp.

This brief narrative describes engagements in the Pacific Theater during the year following Pearl Harbor.

V

516.   Van Vechten, Frederick R., Jr., LTJG, "History of USS LCI 542 1943-1945." Ships, n.d. 36 pp.

This well written history is divided into three parts: European, American, and Pacific operations. The author served on the ship during the period between 26 January 1944 and 20 November 1945. The ship made a total of 15 round trips across the English Channel during the Normandy campaign. Returning to America she began conversion to a gunboat for the invasion of Japan. However, with the surrender she was reconverted to a troop carrier. In October 1945, she set sail for the Leyte area where she operated for five months. Lists of ports visited and members of the crew are included.

517.   Van Wyen, Adrian O., "Chronology of Lighter-Than-Air History in the U. S. Navy, 1915-1962." Individual Personnel, 1962. 18 pp.

This is a chronology of both the operational and administrative highlights in the 47-year history of Naval airships.

518.   Van Wyen, Adrian O., "Notes on the Origin of Torpedo Attack in the United States Navy." Individual Personnel, 1948. 6 pp.

A brief discussion of the development of aerial torpedo attack from the first proposal in 1912 to the assignment of carrier-based torpedo and bombing units in 1927.

519. VICKSBURG (CL-86), Aviation Unit, "History of Aviation Unit, U.S.S. VICKSBURG (CL-86)." Ships, 1945. 8 pp.

This brief unit history covers the period from 27 April 1944 to 20 August 1945 during which time this cruiser participated in operations at Iwo Jima, Ulithi, Okinawa, Leyte, and Tokyo Bay.

520. VINCENNES (CL-64), Aviation Unit, "History of Aviation Unit, U.S.S. VINCENNES (CL-64)." Ships, July 1945. 11 pp. Appendices.

This unit history covers the period from October 1943 to July 1945. It is a brief account of service in the Pacific Theater, during which time this cruiser participated in campaigns in the Marianas, Palau, Philippine Islands, Iwo Jima, and Okinawa.

521. Vollbrecht, John, LTJG, "The Ulithi Encyclopedia." Individual Personnel, 1945. 41 pp.

"The Ulithi Encyclopedia" was prepared in guide-book form for personnel assigned to the Atoll. The booklet includes a brief history of the island, discussions of the natives' social structure and life style, and of the flora and fauna on the island, as well as a short account of the unopposed landing in September 1944.

W

522. War Department, Army Service Forces, Office of the Chief Signal Officer, "Expediting Activities of the Office of the Chief Signal Officer, August 1941 - June 1944." Admin. Hist. Appen. Procurement and Material 24, May 1945. 86 pp. Appendices, charts.

    This history traces the genesis, development, and eventual dissolution of this activity in a fully annotated, effectively organized narrative. Special attention is focused on the joint Army-Navy role of the agency.

523. War Department, "Report on the Development of U.S. Postal Censorship During its first year of operation, 1942." Army, 19 January 1943. 253 pp.

    This history describes the development of postal censorship from 1 June 1941, when the President approved a plan for censorship and made it the responsibility of the War Department, to 31 December 1942, when practically all Army officers were relieved of censorship duties. Topics covered include organization, administration, personnel procurement, regulations, planning, and operations.

524. War Shipping Administration, "The United States Merchant Marine at War." Independent Agencies, 1946. 80 pp. Illustrations.

    A generalized account of the role of the merchant marine in World War II.

525.   Ware, Leonard, CDR, "The Normandy Invasion."
Individual Personnel, 8 January 1945. 26 pp.

   This well-written account of the Normandy
Invasion covers the following aspects: the preparations which began two years before 6 June 1944; various problems in landing at Omaha and Utah beaches; the creation of artificial harbors and small-boat harbors; the bombardment of Cherbourg by the fire-support force of the Western Task Force; the buildup in France; a list of personnel and ship casualties during the assault and buildup; and administrative changes in the Commander, Naval Forces, Europe and Commander, 12th Fleet.

526.   Washington Navy Yard, Ordnance and Gunnery
Schools, "Administrative History of the Ordnance and Gunnery Schools, Navy Yard, Washington, D.C." Admin. Hist. Appen. 30 (1), July 1945. 116 pp. Appendices.

   The account traces the administrative development of each department within these schools, beginning soon after the outbreak of World War II.

527.   Watkins, David D., LCDR, "Historical Narrative
of the Senior U.S. Naval Member S.H.A.E.F. Mission to Denmark and Senior U.S. Naval Officer U.S.F.E.T. Mission to Denmark." Naval Forces, 1946. 35 pp.

   This narrative gives a brief account of the activities of the Senior U.S. Naval Member, Supreme Headquarters Allied Expeditionary Forces, Europe Mission in Denmark and Senior U.S. Naval Officer, U.S. Forces European Theater Mission in Denmark immediately following World War II. The study is well-written and contains a table of contents.

528.   Weaver, Robert Kenneth, LTJG (SC), Gordon Hayward Klippel, LTJG (CEC), et al., "Historical Narrative of the First Special U.S. Naval Construction Battalion." Admin. Hist. Appen. 34 (15) (A), 1 July 1945. 32 pp. Photographs.

   The First Special Naval Construction Battalion was organized in late 1942 to meet the Navy's stevedoring needs in the Pacific Theatre. This history traces its inception, development, operations, and return to the United States in mid-1944.

529.   Western Defense Command, "Japanese Free Balloons and Related Incidents." U.S. Army, 1945. 55 pp. Illustrations.

   This detailed and technical intelligence study pertains to the arrival of Japanese incendiary balloons in the Western United States from 4 November 1944 to 10 February 1945.

530.   Whidbey Island, Washington, Naval Air Station, "History of the CIC [Combat Information Center] Team Training Center, U.S. Naval Air Station, Whidbey Island, Washington." Admin. Hist. Appen. 21 (17), 5 September 1945. 12 pp. Appendices.

   The well documented and readable narrative, which covers the period from 5 July 1943 to mid-1945, includes course schedules and outlines.

531.   White Oak Naval Ordnance Laboratory, "The History of the Naval Ordnance Laboratory 1918-1945." Shore Establishment, n.d. 570 pp. Appendices, illustrations.

This history is divided into three parts: the administrative history dwells in a large degree on personnel problems and the organization at the laboratory at White Oak, Maryland; the history of the training program shows the development of this program and subjects covered; and the scientific history gives a detailed account of various research and development programs to design mines, depth charges, mine countermeasures, and various other weapons.

532.   WISCONSIN (BB-64), Aviation Unit, "History of Aviation Unit, U.S.S. WISCONSIN (BB-64)." Ships, 1945. 7 pp.

This short unit history covers the period from 1 March 1944 to 1 August 1945, during which time this battleship participated in operations at Ulithi, Okinawa, and Hokkaido.

533.   WOLVERINE (IX-64), "History of U.S.S. WOLVERINE (IX-64)." Ships, 1945. 5 pp. Illustrations.

This history covers the period from 12 August 1942-1 April 1945, when the ship was used as a training carrier on Lake Michigan. Photographs of severe ice conditions in the winter of 1945 are included.

534.   Worthington, Joseph M., RADM, "History of the U.S.S. BENHAM (DD-397)." Ships, 1965. 44 pp.

This history consists of three articles (one of which was printed in Shipmate magazine) giving an interesting account of the wartime career of the U.S.S. BENHAM (DD-397) which the author commanded in 1941-1942.

535.   Worthington, Joseph M., RADM, "The Story of Destroyer Squadron Fifty-Seven, World War II." Type Commands, 1968. 39 pp.

Rear Admiral Worthington was the squadron's commander from 15 January 1945 to 3 November 1945. This account is based largely on his war diary and individual ships histories. All ships of the squadron saw duty after late 1944 in the Aleutians, as radar pickets at Okinawa, and in the home waters of Japan during the waning days of the war.

536.   Wright Jerauld, ADM, "An Evening with Admiral Jerauld Wright." Individual Personnel, 4 October 1966. 27 pp.

This contains recollections and opinions of Admiral Jerauld Wright, a member of General Eisenhower's Staff in 1942, Supreme Allied Commander, Atlantic in the 1950's, and U. S. Ambassador to China in 1963, as given during a personal interview with Professor Robert Langdon during the Distinguished Visitors Program of Annapolis.

X - Y - Z

537.　　Yards and Docks, Bureau, "Construction Battalions in the Invasion of Normandy." Shore Establishment, 1944. 49 pp.

　　The draft covers the organization and accomplishments of the Navy's Construction Battalions participating in the Normandy Invasion. A detailed discussion is given of the development and installation of the man-made harbors built to facilitate the provision of supplies for the invasion force.

538.　　Yards and Docks, Bureau, "Office of Director, Atlantic Division, Report on Establishment and Construction of Naval Facilities in Bermuda." Shore Establishment, 1946. 109 pp. Index.

　　The narrative includes personnel, chronological, and financial information describing the construction of the Bermuda bases, the number of personnel involved, and costs, as well as a discussion of disposal of surplus material at the end of World War II. The bibliography serves as a useful guide to further study.

539.　　Zimmerman, John L., CAPT, USMC, "The Second Marine Division." USMC, n.d. 24 pp.

　　This is a brief outline history of the unit from February 1941 through 1945, during which time it participated in the Guadalcanal, Gilbert Islands, Saipan, and Tinian campaigns.

GLOSSARY OF ABBREVIATIONS

Abbreviation	Name
ADM	Admiral
Admin. Hist. Appen.	Administrative History Appendices Collection (Operational Archives, Naval History Division)
AFHQ	Allied Force Headquarters
AGC	Amphibious Force Flagship
AKA	Attack Cargo Ship
APA	Attack Transport
APD	High Speed Transport
AR	Repair Ship
Arch.	Archipelago
ASW	Antisubmarine Warfare
ATB	Amphibious Training Base
AVP	Small Seaplane Tender
BB	Battleship
BUAER	Bureau of Aeronautics
BUSANDA	Bureau of Supplies and Accounts

CA	Heavy Cruiser
CAPT	Captain
CASU	Carrier Aircraft Service Unit
CB	Large Cruiser
CBMU	Construction Battalion Maintenance Unit
CDR	Commander (rank)
CE 2	Construction Electrician, Second Class
CEC	Civil Engineering Corps
CIC	Combat Information Center
CINCPAC	Commander in Chief, U. S. Pacific Fleet
CINCPAC/POA	Commander in Chief, U. S. Pacific Fleet and Pacific Ocean Areas
CL	Light Cruiser
CNO	Chief of Naval Operations
COL	Colonel
COM	Commander (position)
COMNAVNAW	Commander U. S. Naval Forces Northwest African Waters

COMO	Commodore
CPO	Chief Petty Officer
CTF	Commander Task Force
CV	Aircraft Carrier
CVE	Aircraft Carrier, Escort
DCNO	Deputy Chief of Naval Operations
DD	Destroyer
DIV.	Division
ENS	Ensign
FGN	Federal German Navy
FRUPAC	Fleet Radio Unit, Pacific
FY	Fiscal Year
GROPAC	Group Pacific
HC	Hospital Corps
I.J.N.	Imperial Japanese Navy
Is.	Island
IX	Unclassified Miscellaneous Ship
JCS	Joint Chiefs of Staff
LCDR	Lieutenant Commander

LCI	Landing Craft, Infantry
LCS(L)(3)	Landing Craft, Support (Large) (Mark III)
LSM	Landing Ship, Medium
LST	Landing Ship, Tank
LT	Lieutenant
LTA	Lighter-than-Air Craft
LTCOL	Lieutenant Colonel
LTJG	Lieutenant (Junior Grade)
MC	Medical Corps
MGEN	Major General
MTB	Motor Torpedo Boat
NAAS	Naval Auxiliary Air Station
ND	Naval District
N.O.B.	Naval Operating Base
NROTC	Naval Reserve Officer Training Corps
NTS	Naval Training School
OEG	Operations Evaluation Group
ONI	Office of Naval Intelligence

PBY	Twin-Engine Navy Patrol-bomber
PhM1	Pharmacist's Mate, First Class
PT	Motor Torpedo Boat
RADM	Rear Admiral
RN	Royal Navy
SC	Supply Corps
SERVRON SOPAC	Service Squadron, South Pacific Force
SHAEF	Supreme Headquarters, Allied Expeditionary Force
SOLANT	South Atlantic Command
SOPAC	South Pacific Area and Forces
SPATU	South Pacific Aircraft Training Unit
S.S.	Steamship (Merchant Ship)
SS	Submarine
SUBRON	Submarine Squadron
SUSNLO	Senior United States Naval Liaison Officer
TM1(SS)	Torpedoman First Class, Submarines

UDT	Underwater Demolition Team
U.S.	United States
USA	United States Army
USAF	United States Air Force
USFET	United States Forces, European Theater
USMC	United States Marine Corps
USMCWR	United States Marine Corps Women's Reserve
USN	United States Navy
USNTS	United States Naval Training School
U.S.S.	United States Ship (Naval)
VADM	Vice Admiral
VCS	Cruiser-Scouting Squadron
V-J Day	Victory over Japan (14 August 1945)
VMB	Marine Medium and Heavy Patrol Bomber Squadron
VMF	Marine Fighter Squadron
VMSB	Marine Scout Bombing Squadron

VS	Navy Shore-based Scouting Squadron
VT fuse	Variable Time Fuse
WAVES	Women Accepted for Volunteer Emergency Service (Women's Reserve)
WR	Women's Reserve
Y3c(T)	Yeoman, Third Class, Temporary Active Reserve

SUBJECT INDEX

(Note: This index refers to entry numbers, rather than page numbers. In most cases, authors are not indexed, since they appear alphabetically in the checklist.)

A

Admiralty Islands, 246

Advanced Bases, 32, 151, 231, 255, 353, 386-88, 465, 486

    Construction, 1, 100, 115, 407

    Units, 228, 238, 407, 485

Advanced Base Unit 2, 228

Aircraft Carriers, 141, 347, 368-69, 380, 438, 449, 459, 533

Air Force, U. S. Army, 2-4, 27, 35, 216, 424, 487

Airships; see lighter-than-air

Air Stations, air facilities, and air bases, 13, 117, 142, 201, 257, 357, 390, 530

    Brazil, 49, 156, 163, 213, 227, 370, 395

U.S.S. ALABAMA, 456

Alaska, 10, 11, 309, 514

Aleutian Islands, 106, 210, 285, 535

    Attu Is., 10, 372, 514

    Kiska Is., 11, 245, 308, 367, 514

Algiers, 450

Allied Commands, 63, 66, 109, 147, 148, 190, 226; see also Supreme Headquarters, Allied Expeditionary Force

Allied Commission, Austria, 34

Allied Commission, Italy, 148

Allied Force Headquarters, 66

Ambridge, Pa., 350

American Bridge Company, 350

Ammunition Depots, Naval, 104, 127

Amphibious Forces, 248, 252-54, 353, 360, 511, 512

    Combat operations, 2, 14-17, 197, 244-47, 249-51, 265, 418, 419, 467-77

    Training, 18, 19, 139, 172, 218, 284, 313, 314, 466, 478-80

Anguar Is. (Carolines), 496, 498

Ani Jima (Bonins), 514

Annual Reports, 32, 82, 319

    Discontinued commands, 33, 41, 43, 341, 403, 444, 513

Antiaircraft, 354, 356

Antisubmarine Warfare, 113, 129, 271, 275, 435, 449, 457; see also Submarines

Anti-Submarine Warfare Training Center, 113

Anzio, Italy, 139, 210

Armed Guards, 76, 198

Army-Navy Composite Task Force, Ascension Is., 485

Army, U.S., 28, 143, 160, 173, 217, 241, 265, 282, 401, 448, 485, 522, 523

    Aviation, 2-4, 27, 35, 216, 424, 487

    Intelligence activities, 10, 11, 24-26, 529

Aruba Is., 262

Ascension Is., 485

Atlantic Fleet, U.S., 32, 536

Atomic Test Site, Bikini Atoll, 95

Attachés, Naval, 54, 60, 149, 188, 310, 423

Attu Is. (Aleutians), 10, 372, 514

Australia, 151, 246, 266, 355

Austria, 34

Auxiliary Ships, 56, 185, 193, 234, 260, 291, 394, 404

Avalanche, Operation, 197; see also Salerno

Aviation, 35, 36, 51, 116, 117, 152, 216, 243, 352, 459, 461, 518; see also Aircraft Carriers

    Combat operations, 2, 3, 5, 27, 152, 181, 233, 267-69, 347, 355, 464

    Unit histories, 1, 7, 74, 110, 158, 159, 180-83, 201, 428, 454, 487

Aviation Units (scouting and observation)

    Battleships, 8, 61, 209, 272, 280, 307, 427, 532

    Cruisers, 9, 20, 30, 80, 92, 153, 184, 279, 294, 301, 340, 346, 348, 358, 365, 367, 372, 382, 391, 396, 484, 519, 520

Azores, Naval Forces, 37

B

Babcock and Wilcox Company, 40

Balboa, Panama Canal Zone, 134

Balikpapan, Borneo, 470

Balloons, Japanese, 529

Bandoeng, Java, 276

Base Depot, Russell Islands, 164

Bases and operating facilities, Naval,

    Atlantic, 37, 38, 50, 67, 128, 208, 229, 275, 295, 306, 374, 375, 397, 448, 453, 512, 538

    Pacific, 62, 134, 143, 214, 223, 224, 231, 232, 236, 239, 316, 339, 379, 383, 393, 464, 489

Batavia, Java, 276

Battle Narratives, 210, 298, 514, 515

Battleships, 8, 61, 137, 209, 272, 280, 307, 427, 532

Belgium, 147

U.S.S. BENHAM, 534

Bering Sea, 299

Bering Sea Patrol, 87

Berkeley, Calif., 300

Bermuda, 538

Bethlehem Steel Company, 366

Biak Is., New Guinea, 160, 294

Bikini Atoll (Marshalls), 95

Bilibid Prison, Philippines, 191, 225, 274, 398

Biscay, Bay of, 443

Bislig Bay, Philippines, 514

Bismark Archipelago, 290

    New Britain Is., 56, 246, 266, 418, 458

    Manus Is., 14, 472, 473, 476, 495

U.S.S. BLOCK ISLAND, 449

Boat Operating and Repair Unit, Guadalcanal, 255

Bonin Islands, 157, 500, 514

Bordeaux, France, 48

Borneo, 90, 294, 418, 470, 504

Boston, Mass., 119

Bougainville, Is. (Solomons), 95, 96, 180, 210, 265, 496

Boulder, Colo., 300

Bowdoin College, 58

Brazil, 165

    Bases and operating facilities, 38, 50, 67, 295, 374, 397

    Air stations, facilities, and bases, 49, 156, 163, 213, 227, 370, 395

Bremen, Germany, 175

Bremerhaven, Germany, 175

Bridgeport, Conn., 189

British; see Great Britain

Brunei Bay, Borneo, 294

Buffalo, N.Y., 125

Bureau of Aeronautics, 152

Bureau of Medicine and Surgery, 273, 274

Bureau of Navigation, 341; see also Bureau of Personnel

Bureau of Ordnance, 57

Bureau of Personnel, 342, 343; see also Bureau of Navigation

Bureau of Supplies and Accounts, 446, 447

Bureau of Yards and Docks, 448

C

Cabanatuan, Philippines, 274

California, University of, 300

Camp Lejeune, N.C., 218

Canacao, Philippines, 108, 225

U.S.S. CANOPUS, 381

Caroline Islands, 488, 498, 514, 520

    Peleliu Is., 14, 247, 266, 339, 458, 494, 496

    Truk Is., 8, 279, 514

    Ulithi Atoll, 477, 488, 489, 514, 521

    Yap Is., 473, 488, 493

Casablanca, French Morocco, 450

Chemical Warfare, 342

Cherbourg, France, 525

Chicago Bridge and Iron Company, 81

Chichi Jima (Bonins), 514

Chief of Naval Operations, 82

    Office of, 5, 35, 36, 47, 116, 198, 210-12, 240

China, 161, 418, 452, 455, 468, 536

China, Burma, India Theater, 27

Ciudad Trujillo, Dominican Republic, 60

Civil Affairs, 143; see also Military Government

U.S.S. CLAXTON, 194

Cleveland Diesel Engine, General Motors Corporation, 83

Coast Guard, U.S., 13, 85-89

Colorado, University of, 300

Combat Information Centers, 31, 311, 351, 390, 530

Combat Narratives; see Battle Narratives

Combined Chiefs of Staff, 109

Commander (Komandorski) Islands, 299

Committee on Public Information, 22

Communications, 58, 203, 229, 261, 314, 403, 481; see also Loran, Radar

    Activities, 72, 121, 264, 323-25, 522

Construction Battalion Maintenance Unit 518, 255

Construction Battalion Maintenance Unit 520, 255

Construction Battalion Maintenance Unit 533, 255

Construction Battalions, 95-101, 448, 528, 537

Convoy and Escort Operations, 259, 271, 345, 377, 453

Coordinator of Research and Development, 171; see also Research and Development

Coral Sea Battle, 210, 298, 358

Coronado, Calif., 466

Corregidor Is., Philippines, 246, 282, 355, 381

Creel Committee, 22

Cruisers, 9, 184

    Heavy, 80, 153, 279, 301, 340, 348, 358, 365, 391

    Light, 20, 30, 92, 294, 346, 367, 372, 382, 396, 484, 519, 520

Cuba, 20, 194

Culebra Is., Puerto Rico, 172

Cutters, Coast Guard, 86

D

Dartmouth College V-12 Unit, 118

Defense, Department of, 315

U.S.S. DELTA, 193

Denmark, 88, 89, 147, 527

Destroyers, 79, 90, 112, 113, 194, 259, 534

Destroyer Squadron Fifty-Seven, 535

Dieppe Raid, 188

Distribution, Director of, Fifth Naval District, 128

District Material Office, Third Naval District, 123

Districts, Naval, 117-34, 242, 306

Dominican Republic, 60

Doolittle Raid; see Halsey-Doolittle Raid

Dragoon, Operation, 197; see also Southern France Invasion

Drydocks, Naval, 196, 462

E

Eighth Fleet, U.S., 139, 375, 450

Emergency Management, Office of, 240

Empress Augusta Bay, Bougainville, 210

Engano, Cape, Philippines, 514

England; see Great Britain

Eniwetok Atoll (Marshalls), 200, 224, 472, 476, 477

    Combat operations, 26, 247, 249, 250, 514

U.S.S. ENTERPRISE, 158

Esperance, Cape, Guadalcanal, 210

Espiritu Santo Is. (New Hebrides), 142, 143, 231, 428

Europe, Naval Forces, 34, 145-49

Ewa, Oahu, Hawaiian Islands, 201

F

Fairbanks, Morse and Company, 52

Fauripik Is. (Carolines), 488

Field Production Division, Third Naval District, 123

Fifteenth Naval District, 134

Fifth Marine Amphibious Corps, 265

Fifth Marine Division, 78, 157

Fifth Naval District, 128, 129, 306

Fighting Squadron Six, 183

Fiji Islands, 359

First Marine Aircraft Wing, 180

First Marine Division, 266, 458

First Naval District, 117-19

First Special U.S. Naval Construction Battalion, 528

Fleet Air Wing Seventeen, 110

Fleet Hospital 108, 255; see also Medical Services

Fleet Organization, 1919-1941, 237

Fleet Radio Unit, Pacific, 325

Flight Gridiron, Operation, 355

Fort Miflin Ammunition Depot, Fourth Naval District, 127

Fort Pierce, Fla., 509

Forward Area, Central Pacific, 68-74

Foster Wheeler Corporation, 65, 105

Fourteenth Naval District, 132, 133

Fourth Marine Division, 77

Fourth Naval District, 127, 242

France, 48, 55, 168-69, 188, 197, 257, 432, 525; see also Normandy Invasion, Southern France Invasion

France, Naval Forces, 168, 169

France, Naval Task Group, 168, 169

French Frigate Shoals, Hawaiian Islands, 13

French Morocco, 139

FRUPAC, 325

G

Gaeta, Italy, 210

General Motors, 83, 162

Germany, 67, 150, 175, 176

    Armed Forces, 89, 129, 174, 176, 212, 262, 371, 378, 439, 457

Germany, Naval Forces, 174-76

Gilbert Islands, 8, 210, 270, 271, 454, 472, 514, 539

    Tarawa Atoll, 26, 97, 281, 358, 490

Gloucester, Cape, New Britain, 246

Goodenough Is., New Guinea, 246

Great Britain, 86, 145, 188, 241, 276, 353, 377, 512

    Allied cooperation, 109, 149, 226, 443, 448

S.S. GREATER BUFFALO, 380

Greenland, 88, 453

U.S.S. GREER, 453

U.S.S. GREGORY, 260

Group Pacific Twelve, 238

Guadalcanal Campaign, 177, 360; see also Solomon Islands

    Combat operations, 14, 180, 182, 210, 247, 259, 266, 298, 458, 539

    Logistic support operations, 98, 99, 101, 255, 472, 476

Guam, Battle of; see also Mariana Islands

    Combat operations, 14, 247, 249, 250, 281, 492, 494

    Logistic support operations, 56, 95, 402, 471, 472

Guam Is. (Marianas), 46, 221, 264

Guantanamo Bay, Cuba, 20

Guerrilla Warfare, 161, 420

H

Halsey-Doolittle Raid, 27, 210

Harbor Entrance Control Post, Boston, 119

Harvard University, 300

Havana, Cuba, 194

Hawaiian Islands, 13, 248-50, 433, 478, 480, 509; see also Pearl Harbor

    Oahu Is., 132, 201, 311, 312

U.S.S. HELENA, 167

Hingham, Mass., 104

Hokadate, Japan, 506

Hokkaido, Japan, 532

Holland, 147; see also Netherlands

Hollandia, New Guinea, 56, 246

Honshu Raid, 9

Hoquiam, Wash., 318

Hospitals; see Medical Services

Husky, Operation, 197; see also Sicily

I

Iceland, 208, 453

Ie Shima (Ryukyus), 238

Indo-China, 293

Industrial Managers, 39, 130, 195, 304, 392, 405

Industry Cooperation Division, Procurement and Material Office, 362

Inspection District, Pittsburgh, Pa., 349

Inspectors of Machinery, 40, 52, 65, 83, 105, 144

Inspectors of Naval Material, 125, 189, 302, 349

Inspectors of Ordnance, 399

Intelligence, 10, 11, 25, 26, 148, 149, 157, 176, 267-69, 529

    Activities, 5, 122, 131, 210-12, 308, 323, 325, 420, 425

Interviews, 59, 155, 438, 536

Ireland, Northern, 448

Ironton, Ohio, 350

Italy, 89, 94, 139, 148, 197, 210, 212, 445; see also Sicily

Iwo Jima, Battle of; see also Ryukyu Islands

    Combat operations, 9, 30, 77, 78, 247, 256, 281, 499, 500, 501, 514, 519, 520

    Logistic support operations, 256, 415, 467, 471, 472, 476

J

Japanese Home Islands Campaign, 19, 211, 480, 514

    Air operations, 5, 9, 30, 80, 464, 487, 519, 532

    Surface-ship operations, 247, 250, 415, 467, 469, 471, 535

    Underwater demolition operations, 491, 493, 495, 503, 504, 506, 508

Japan Sea, 211

Java, 276

Java Sea, 210

Jinsen, Korea, 497, 507

Johns Hopkins University, 222

Joint Army-Navy Board, 109

Joint Chiefs of Staff, 109, 190

Joint Overseas Operations, 296

K

U.S.S. KEARNY, 453

Key West, Fla., 275

Kiriwina Is. (Trobriands), 246

Kiska Is. (Aleutians), 11, 245, 308, 367, 514

Kolombangara Is. (Solomons), 210

Komandorski Is. (Commanders), 299

Korea, 418, 497, 499, 507

Kwajelein Atoll (Marshalls), 8, 26, 77, 210, 232

L

L'Aber Vrach, France, 257

Lae, New Guinea, 210

Landing Craft, 234, 235, 244-54, 292, 516; see also Amphibious Forces

U.S.S. LCI-542, 516

U.S.S. LSM-36, 244

Lejeune, Camp, N.C., 218

Lend-Lease, 86, 199, 226, 421

U.S.S. LEXINGTON, 438

Leyte Gulf, Battle of, 207, 298, 514; see also Philippines Campaign

    Combat operations, 2, 45, 112, 246, 279, 456, 516, 519

    Logistic support operations, 402, 470-72, 476, 491, 492, 494, 496-98

Leyte Gulf, Philippines, 239, 252

Liaison Officer, Italy, Senior U.S., 148

Lighter-than-Air Craft, 6, 132, 426, 517

Lingayen Gulf, Philippines, 112, 244, 246, 402, 468, 496, 497, 501; see also Philippines Campaign

Loch Ryan, Scotland, 448

Logistic Support, 32, 68, 70, 120, 216, 323, 447, 450; see also Service Forces

    Procurement, 173, 219, 446

    Supply bases, 104, 164, 169, 239, 255, 305, 486

    Units, 4, 28, 40, 240, 283, 326-32, 393, 402, 406-17, 422

Londonderry, Northern Ireland, 448

London, England, 145, 149, 188, 241

Loran, 13, 58; see also Communications, Radar

Lough Erne, Northern Ireland, 448

Luzon, Philippines, 8, 268, 281, 470, 473, 514; see also Philippines Campaign

M

Mail; see Postal Services

Majuro Atoll (Marshalls), 210

Makassar Straits, Battle of, 90

Makin Atoll (Gilberts), 472, 514

Maloelap Atoll (Marshalls), 279

Malta, 259

Manila Bay, Philippines, 282

Manila, Philippines, 192, 225, 398

Manus Is. (Bismark Arch.), 14, 472, 473, 476, 495

Maracaibo, Venezuela, 262

Marcus Is., 210, 493

Mare Is.; see Vallejo, Calif.

Mariana Islands, 46, 221, 264, 383, 463, 464; see also Guam, Battle of, Saipan, Battle of

 Tinian Is., 77, 247, 463, 464, 473, 493-95, 539

Marianas, Battle of, 210, 248, 333, 469, 491, 514

 Air operations, 8, 233, 520

Marines, U.S., 93, 164, 204, 205, 218, 265, 460

 Air units, 180-82, 201, 267-69, 454

 Ground-combat units, 77, 78, 134, 157, 192, 266, 425, 437, 458, 539

Maritime Commission, 91

Mark 15 (Norden) Bomb Sight, 57

Marshall Islands, 26, 95, 97, 210, 270, 271, 279, 333, 454, 490, 493

 Eniwetok Atoll, 26, 200, 224, 247, 249, 250, 472, 476, 477, 514

 Kwajelein Atoll, 8, 26, 77, 210, 232

Maui, Hawaiian Islands, 509

Medical Services, 136, 146, 229, 273, 274, 330, 352

 Facilities, 108, 132, 191, 192, 225, 241, 255, 303, 398, 412

Mediterranean, 66, 212, 286, 371, 375, 376

    Landings, 193, 210, 450

Merchant Shipping, 76, 89, 129, 176, 377, 524; see also Convoy and Escort Operations

Merritt, Chapman, and Scott, 385

Miami, Fla., 130

Midway, Battle of, 210, 298, 369, 514

    Unit histories, 158, 182, 183, 358

Miflin, Fort; see Fort Miflin Ammunition Depot

Military Government, 297

    Activities, 46, 69, 143, 176, 221, 270, 330, 333

Milne Bay, New Guinea, 236

Mindanao, Philippines, 244, 470

Mindoro, Philippines, 110, 246, 470

Mine Assembly Depot Number Four, Tinian, 463

Mine Warfare, 242, 275, 277, 278, 452, 463, 487, 531

Morocco; see French Morocco

Motor Torpedo Boats, 21, 106, 285-90, 483

Mt. Vernon, Ohio, 350

Munda, New Guinea, 210

Munitions Board, Army-Navy, 217

N

Naples, Italy, 445

National Defense Advisory Commission and Office of Production Management, 91, 424

Nauru Is., 514

Naval Advisor, Military Government of Germany, 176

Naval Forces, U.S., 34, 37, 145-49, 174-76, 168, 169, 309, 450

Naval Group China, 161

Naval Landing Force Equipment Depot, Guadalcanal, 255

Naval Missions in Europe, 147, 150, 170, 310, 527

Naval Transportation Service, 12, 393

Navy, Department of, 361-64, 421

Navy Salvage Service, 385

Navy Yards; see Shipyards

Netherlands, 170; see also Holland

Neville Is., Pittsburgh, Pa., 350

New Britain (Bismark Arch.), 56, 180, 210, 266, 418, 458

New Caledonia, 100, 430, 432, 476

Newfoundland, 453

New Georgia Is. (Solomons), 180, 182, 210, 290

New Guinea, 56, 236, 246, 290, 418, 470, 472

New Hebrides Islands, 142, 143, 231, 428

New London, Conn., 229

New Orleans, La., 106

New York, N. Y., 123, 126, 302, 385

New Zealand, 276, 359, 429, 465

U.S.S. NOA, 56

Norden Bomb Sight, 57

Norfolk, Va., 128, 217, 304-306

Normandy Invasion, 136, 145, 146, 197, 378, 448, 514, 525; see also France

    Participating units, 4, 111, 136, 146, 516, 537

North Africa, 66, 193, 197, 210, 368, 450; see also Torch, Operation

Northern Force, U.S., 10

Northhampton, Mass., 436

North Pacific, Naval Forces, 309

Northwest African Waters, Naval Forces, 450

Norway, 147, 310

O

Oahu, Hawaiian Islands, 132, 311, 312

Office of Emergency Management, 240

Ohio River, 215

Okinawa, Battle of, 96, 103, 281, 287, 535, 415

    Air operations, 8, 255, 267, 279, 280, 514, 519, 520, 532

    Amphibious operations, 14-18, 234, 235, 256, 266, 425, 458, 467, 469, 471, 473-75, 477

    Underwater demolition operations, 492, 495, 499, 500-503, 505, 507

Okinawa Is. (Ryukus), 316, 505

Oran, Algeria, 450

Ordnance, 230, 526

    Ammunition, 68, 104, 127, 217, 277

    Research and development, 57, 152, 222, 352, 401, 531

Overlord, Operation, 4, 197; see also Normandy Invasion

P

Pacific Fleet, U.S., 319-37, 438

    Subordinate commands, 41, 43, 113, 403, 406-13, 417, 442, 444

Palau Is. (Carolines), 514, 520

Palembang, Sumatra, 276

Panama Canal Zone, 134

U.S.S. PANAY, 455

Pasay School, Philippines, 274

Pearl Harbor, 113, 132, 338, 411, 412, 433; see also Hawaiian Islands

    Attack, 167, 190, 201, 210, 382, 514

Peleliu Is. (Carolines), 14, 247, 266, 339, 458, 494, 496

Perth, Australia, 355

Philippine Coast Artillery Command, 282

Philippines, 239, 282, 290, 355, 381, 460

    Japanese occupation, 108, 191, 192, 225, 274, 398, 420

Philippines Campaign, 160, 207, 298

    Air operations, 2, 8, 30, 110, 185, 268, 269, 279, 519, 520

    Amphibious operations, 14-16, 244, 246-250, 252, 281, 418

    Surface-ship operations, 112, 185, 290, 402, 456, 468, 470-73, 476, 514

    Underwater demolition operations, 491-94, 496-98, 501

Philippine Sea Frontier, 290, 345

Photographic and Reproduction Unit, 431

Physical Fitness, 186

Ponape Is. (Carolines), 514

Port Directors, 107, 126, 200

Portland, Me., 217

Port Operations, 48, 119, 126, 175, 238, 445

Ports and Bases France, (TF-125), 169, 376

Ports and Bases, Germany, (TF-126), 175

Postal Services, 71, 165, 283, 321, 523

Princeton University, 297

Prisoners of War, 274, 276, 293

    Medical treatment, 108, 191, 192, 225, 273, 398

Public Information Offices, 22, 315, 335

Puerto Rico, 172

Pullman-Standard Car Manufacturing Company, 81

R

Rabaul, New Britain, 180, 210

Radar, 58, 202, 204, 352, 408, 411, 481; see also Communications, Loran

Recife, Brazil, 67, 165

Research and Development, 171, 203, 204, 351, 352, 483

    Ordnance, 57, 152, 222, 401, 531

Reserves, Naval, 118, 194, 205, 341, 436

Roi Namur Is. (Marshalls), 493

Roll-Up, Operation, 413

Rosneath, Scotland, 448

Russell Islands, 164, 379

Russia; see Soviet Union

Ryukyu Islands, 23, 238, 316, 500, 505; see also Okinawa, Battle of

S

Saigon Raid, 293

St. George, Cape, New Ireland Is., 514

Saipan, Battle of,

    Combat operations, 8, 14, 77, 210, 247, 249, 281, 493-95, 539

    Logistic support operations, 56, 402, 472, 473

Saipan Is. (Marianas), 383

Salamaua, New Guinea, 210

Salerno, 94, 139, 210; see also Avalanche, Operation

Salvage, 385, 445

Samar, Philippines, 239, 281, 460, 514

Samoa, 386-88

San Clemente Is., Calif., 172, 390

San Diego, Calif., 217, 480

San Francisco, Calif., 29, 76, 196, 392, 393, 481, 482

San Pedro, Calif., 107, 172, 195, 394

Santa Cruz Islands, 210, 358, 395

Sao Luiz, Brazil, 227

Satawan Atoll (Carolines), 514

Savo Is. Battle, 210, 298

Schools, Naval; see Training

Scotland, 448

Seabees; see Construction Battalions

Second Marine Aircraft Wing, 182

Second Marine Division, 539

Service Force, Pacific, 41, 283, 406-13, 422; see also Logistic Support

Service Force, U.S. Seventh Fleet, 414

Seventh Fleet, U.S., 102, 290, 414, 420

Seventh Naval District, 130

Shipyards and Shipbuilding, 39, 42, 44, 75, 81, 84, 91, 114, 123, 130, 196, 206, 255, 263, 292, 304, 317, 338, 384, 405, 526; see also Supervisor of Shipbuilding

Sicily, 24, 25, 139, 210, 228; see also Husky, Operation, Italy

Singapore, 276

Sixth Army, U.S., 160

Sixth Marine Division, 425, 437

Smith College, 436

Society Islands, 55

Solomon Islands, 62, 177, 210, 514; see also Guadalcanal Campaign

    Bougainville Is., 95, 96, 180, 210, 265, 496

    New Georgia Is., 180, 182, 290

    Tulagi Is., 210, 266, 458, 486

Sorol Is. (Carolines), 488

South Atlantic Campaign, 166

South China Sea, 514

U.S.S. SOUTH DAKOTA, 456

Southern France Invasion, 139; see also Dragoon, Operation, France

Soviet Union, 315, 423

Special Naval Observer, London, 145

Stations, Naval, 55, 275

U.S.S. STERETT, 259

Subic Bay, Philippines, 252, 282, 498

Submarines, 135, 151, 229, 439, 440, 444; see also Anti-submarine Warfare

    Combat operations, 45, 53, 129, 210, 262, 371, 420, 434, 441-43

Sumatra, 276

Supervisor of Shipbuilding,

    Eastern U.S., 21, 42, 44, 84, 114, 215, 344, 350, 366, 399, 400, 451

    Western U.S., 81, 138, 317, 384

Supply Depot, Naval, Norfolk, Va., 305

Supreme Headquarters, Allied Expeditionary Force, 147, 170, 310, 527; see also Allied Commands

Surigao Straits Battle, 185, 514; see also Philippines Campaign

T

Tacoma, Wash., 384

Tampa Shipbuilding Company, 451

Tarawa Atoll (Gilberts), 26, 97, 281, 358, 490

Task Force 125, 169, 376

Task Force 126, 175

Task Group 96.3, 271

Task Unit 55.1.3, 103

Tassafaronga, Guadalcanal, 210

Terminal Is., San Francisco, Calif., 196

Third Amphibious Force, 360

Third Fleet, U.S., 9, 80, 514

Third Marine Division, 265

Third Naval Construction Brigade, 102

Third Naval District, 120-26

37th Division, U.S. Army, 265

Tinian Is. (Marianas), 77, 247, 463, 464, 473, 493-95, 539

Todd Pacific Shipyards, 384

Tokyo Bay, Japan, 504, 519

Tokyo Raid, 210; see also Halsey-Doolittle Raid

Torch, Operation, 197; see also North Africa

Torpedo Boats; see Motor Torpedo Boats

Training, 82, 93, 106, 118, 133, 140, 170, 229, 342, 343, 368, 394, 428, 531

    Naval training centers, 31, 76, 113, 206, 311, 312, 318, 354, 356, 389, 462, 482, 530

    Naval training schools, 58, 162, 202, 261, 297, 300, 306, 373, 404, 408, 411, 436, 481, 526

Transport Division Twenty, 472

Transport Division Twenty-One, 472

Transport Squadron Sixteen, 256, 474

Transport Squadron Twelve, 402

Treasure Is., San Francisco, Calif., 29, 76, 481, 482

U.S.S. TREPANG, 434

Trident Conference, 190

Truk Is. (Carolines), 8, 279, 514

Tulagi Is. (Solomons), 210, 266, 458, 486

Tutuila, Samoa, 387

Twelfth Fleet, U.S., 145, 525

Twelfth Naval District, 131

U

Underwater Demolition Teams; see Guam, Iwo Jima, Japanese Home Islands Campaign, Okinawa, Philippines Campaign, Saipan

Ulithi Atoll (Carolines), 477, 488, 489, 514, 521

United Kingdom; see Great Britain

United States Fleet, 237, 513-15

United States Forces, European Theater, 147, 170

Upolu Is. (Samoa), 388

Utility Air Group, 74

V

V-12 Unit, Dartmouth College, 118

Vallejo, Calif., 217, 263

Vella Lavella Is. (Solomons), 210

Venezuela, 262

Vila - Stanmore, New Hebrides Islands, 210

VMB-613, 454

VMF-111, 454

VMSB-331, 454

VPB-144, 454

VS-66, 454

W

Wake Is., 182, 210, 220, 294, 514

War Plans, 226, 336

War Production Board, 75, 292

War Resources Administration, 240

Waterbury, Conn., 189

WAVES, 436

Welfare and Recreation, 72, 337

Western Naval Task Force, 136, 525

Westinghouse Electric Company, 144

Wisconsin, University of, 261

World War I, 22, 48, 144, 179, 257, 363, 377

Y

I.J.N. YAMATO, 137

Yangtze R., China, 452, 455

Yap Is. (Carolines), 473, 488, 493

Yerba Buena Is., San Francisco, Calif., 29

Yokohama, Japan, 249, 508

Yokosuka, Japan, 508

U.S.S. YORKTOWN, 369